A Century of Gamecocks

Memorable Basketball Moments

A portion of the author's royalties are being donated to the University of South Carolina Department of Athletics

Also by Tom Price

The '84 Gamecocks: Fire Ants and Black Magic (1985)

A Century of Gamecocks: Memorable Football Moments (1995)

A Century of Gamecocks: Memorable Baseball Moments (1996)

A Century of Gamecocks

Memorable Basketball Moments

by Tom Price

Summerhouse Press
Columbia, South Carolina

Dedication

This book is dedicated to all the coaches and their players, whose performances on the court created the thrills that made these memorable moments possible, and to the wonderful fans who cheered them on.

FIRST EDITION

ISBN # 1-887714-01-4 (Paperback)

Manufactured in the United States of America
by Wentworth Printing Company, Inc.
Columbia, South Carolina

Contents

Contents

Foreword

There have been many memorable games in the more than 100 year history of University of South Carolina athletics.

Although basketball hasn't been on the scene quite as long as football and baseball, dating back to 1908 at the University of South Carolina, it has contributed much to the history of the Gamecocks.

In *A Century of Gamecocks: Memorable Basketball Moments,* and in volumes covering football and baseball, I have tried to recapture some of those memories.

Long time followers of South Carolina teams may relive past thrills and experiences. For newcomers to the Gamecock scene, accounts of memorable triumphs can be a history lesson.

Whatever, it is hoped *A Century of Gamecocks* will bring reading pleasure to fans of all ages.

There have been many more memorable games than those cited and readers may have other favorites, and may disagree with some of the selections. However, those chronicled on these pages are some of my favorites, either through personal experience or from reading accounts in newspapers and from other sources.

Some memorable moments occurred before I came on the Carolina scene, especially the great teams led by the Tompkins brothers in the 1930s. I was on hand to witness the greatness of Grady Wallace, Ronnie Collins, John Roche, Tom Owens, Kevin Joyce, Alex English, Zam Fredrick and many others who contributed to some outstanding teams and performances. I witnessed the coaching wizardry of Frank McGuire, the creativeness of Chuck Noe, the competitive nature of Bill Foster, George Felton and Eddie Fogler.

I remember the good more vividly than the bad.

* There were the classic battles with the Tar Heels and Blue Devils.

* Frank McGuire vs Al McGuire.

* The Quaker City Classic.

* Madison Square Garden.

* Trips to Milwaukee, Olean, Buffalo, Philadelphia, Durham, Chapel Hill and South Bend. . . .

Those are some memories. There have been many other thrillers in nine decades of Gamecock basketball competition . . . But, these are my favorites.

Thanks to the many journalists whose accounts of happenings on the courts were used as source material and to the Caroliniana Library for making available its microfilm files; to the players and coaches who made these thrills possible. Special thanks to Alex English for allowing use of his poem of tribute to Coach McGuire.

Thanks also to the University of South Carolina Sports Information Office for access to its archives; to the Summerhouse Press for publishing the book, and to those who made available their scrap books, photographs and other material.

TP. . .

A Century of Gamecocks

Memorable Basketball Moments

I

South Carolina

vs

Duke

February 27, 1933--South Carolina 33, Duke 21
(Southern Conference Championship)

at Raleigh, North Carolina

Prior to the 1932-33 season the University of South Carolina's basketball history had been spotty since the Gamecocks began the roundball game October 30, 1908 with a two point, 21-19, loss to Furman.

There had been a few winning seasons, the best being a 14-4 mark in 1927 under Coach Branch Bocock. However, there had been some miserable seasons, the worst being 1-17 under Coach A. W. "Rock" Norman in 1931. The overall record was 139-180-1.

Basketball was slow to catch on. The *Garnet & Black* referred to it as "Sissy Ball" in accounts of the first season. However, with construction of the Carolina Field House in 1927, interest in the sport increased.

The Field House, with a capacity of 3,200, opened February 17-18, 1927 with a two game sweep of the University of Florida, 39-33, and 37-28.

"Playing in the new University Field House before the largest crowds ever witnessing a basketball game in Columbia, the Gamecocks won two games from the University of Florida on successive nights," the yearbook reported.

"One of the University's most serious problems—that of seating comfortably the large crowds which attend indoor athletic contests—was solved for Carolina last year when a huge field house was completed which provides a seating capacity estimated at three thousand...The Field House was completed last spring in time for the final games of the 1927 basketball season to be played," The *Garnet & Black* said. "It ranks with Melton Field (completed in 1926) as one of the greatest constructive strides toward better athletics in the University."

South Carolina's first basketball team in 1908 was referred to as "Sissy Ball" by the student yearbook.—*Garnet & Black*

Bocock, who was athletics director and head football coach in addition to coaching basketball, was quoted by the Associated Press while in Atlanta for the 1927 Southern Conference tournament:

"Basketball is pushing football hard and has already left baseball behind in the race among the collegiate sports for first honors in fan appeal. That it has begun to compete with football as a college sport is due to education of sports fans to the fact that basketball as college men play it, is no women's game."

Bocock's views may have been influenced by the fact that South Carolina had a good team, winning nine of ten conference games and its first two tournament games—32-26 over N.C. State and 32-18 over Georgia Tech before losing to Vanderbilt, 31-25, in the semifinals.

However, Bocock left after that season and, despite the new facility, basketball had four consecutive losing seasons after the 14-4 record in 1927. The Gamecocks were 8-12 in 1928, 8-13 in 1929, 6-10 in 1930, and 1-17 in 1931 before improving to a 9-7 record under Rock Norman in 1932.

There was one significant victory in the 1928-29 season despite the final record of 8-13 under Coach A. W. "Rock" Norman, although the result was more significant to the North Carolina Tar Heels than to the South Carolina Gamecocks.

On January 17, 1929, the Gamecocks defeated North Carolina 28-25 at Chapel Hill. That was the Tar Heels home opener and sixty six years later, through December 1994, the Tar Heels had not lost their first home game of any season since.

North Carolina opened the season with six consecutive road games, losing the first three to Butler, Ohio State and Louisville before winning three straight over Kentucky, Tennessee and Davidson to bring a 3-3 record home for the first game in Chapel Hill.

South Carolina played its first five games on the road, losing twice to Tennessee, to the Jewish Progressive Club in Atlanta, and twice at Georgia before coming home to defeat Presbyterian and Wofford in the first two home games. South Carolina then won at College of Charleston, lost at The Citadel and defeated Clemson in overtime at Columbia, for a 4-6 record before going to Chapel Hill for the Tar Heels home opener.

While South Carolina finished with an 8-13 record that season, North Carolina, 3-4 after losing to the Gamecocks, finished at 17-8 and was second in the Southern Conference with a 12-2 league mark. The Gamecock conference record was 4-9.

Determined to restore the program to winning status, South Carolina recruited four members of the national championship high school team from Athens, Tex., center Dana Henderson, guard John Rowland, and brothers Bennie and Freddie Tompkins.

Freddie Tompkins, the best player among the four, did not enroll until the second semester of the 1931-32 academic year and thus was not eligible for the varsity until February 1, 1933 when he began his sophomore year.

The freshman team of 1932 compiled a 15-0 record and regularly trounced the varsity in scrimmages.

Billy Laval, who had become head football coach and athletics director in 1928, perhaps sensing the Gamecocks were on the verge of a big season in 1933, decided to take over the basketball coaching duties himself with Norman working with the freshmen.

Laval tuned up for a four game season opening road trip by putting three of his Texas imports on display in an exhibition game for the home fans, January 2, 1933, against the Dallas, N. C., YMCA team described in newspaper reports as a group of former college stars who had been "making serious trouble for mighty good teams in the Carolinas." The score was 37-1 at halftime with a final score of 81-8. Dana Henderson led the scoring with 24 points and Bennie Tompkins scored 16.

Laval took his team by train to Tennessee and Kentucky and in its first official outing, "after a nip and tuck battle most of the way, defeated Tennessee 33-29" in Knoxville, the Associated Press reported. Henderson led with 10 points.

The next stop was Sewanee where Henderson scored 19 in a 55-24 win. Vanderbilt, which won the Southern Conference tournament the previous spring before the split which resulted in formation of the Southeastern Conference, derailed the Gamecocks in Nashville, 31-29, and Kentucky, under third year coach Adolph Rupp, won 44-36 at Lexington despite 18 points by Henderson, and South Carolina came home with a 2-2 record.

Henderson scored 19 as the Gamecocks routed Presbyterian 64-30 in the home opener, and improved the record to 4-2 behind Bennie Tompkins' 13 points in a 47-26 win over Clemson before 2,000 fans, "the largest crowd ever" on South Carolina's home court.

Freddie Tompkins joined the varsity after six games as did Grayson Wolf, who had also been ineligible the first part of the season. Their first game was the Gamecocks' second meeting of the season with Kentucky.

A headline in January 29, 1933 editions of *The State* announced: "Carolina Meets Strong Kentucky Cagers Here Thursday."

A sub-head added, "Freddie Tompkins Plays For Birds; Becomes Eligible For Varsity This Week."

The newspaper noted the starting time had been delayed from the usual 8 p. m., until 8:30 "due to the large crowd expected." Kentucky, on a three game trip, downed Vanderbilt 40-29, and Clemson 42-32, on its way to Columbia.

A banner headline in *The State* February 4, 1933, announced: "Carolina hands Kentucky First Southern Defeat of the Year."

Only slightly less prominent, however, was a headline that stated Norma Smith had scored 74 points to give the Monetta High School girls team a district championship with an 80-74 victory over Salley.

In the college game, a 44-38 South Carolina win, Henderson led the scoring with 19 points and Freddie Tompkins, in his varsity debut, scored 17.

John A. Montgomery, in *The State*, wrote: "Kentucky's great basketball team, rated by some experts as the best collegiate team in America, suffered its first defeat to a Southern team last night when the University of South Carolina scored a 44 to 38 win at the University Field House before a crowd of at least 3,500."

Montgomery reported South Carolina took the lead in the first 30 seconds of the game and led the entire contest "except for a brief, one point, Kentucky lead in the second half. Aggie Sale led Kentucky with 15 points.

The victory over Kentucky gave South Carolina a three game winning streak and a 5-2 record. The Gamecocks won the nine regular season games remaining on their schedule to take a 14-2 record and a 12 game win streak into the Southern Conference tournament at Raleigh.

The team defeated Furman 36-26 at Greenville February 22, with Freddie Tompkins scoring a season low six points, and caught a midnight train to Raleigh.

A sports page headline in *The State* announced: "Carolina Smashes Old Liners By One Sided Score to Win First Game," in reporting a 65-28 triumph over Maryland.

The Associated Press account stated, "South Carolina, the favorite, started impressively in the Southern Conference basketball tournament by bowling over Maryland 65 to 28 in the opening round..."

The wire story described the play as "slow for the first few minutes and then the Gamecocks went into action full speed."

The score was 30-10 at halftime and Freddie Tompkins finished with 31 points on 14 field goals and 3 free throws. Henderson added 14.

Things got tougher in the semi-finals with South Carolina surviving two overtimes before outlasting North Carolina 34-32. The Associated Press reported that after the game North Carolina Coach Bo Shepherd bitterly protested a decision by umpire Paul Menton that allowed Bennie Tompkins a second try after he had missed a free throw "because the crowd was yelling during the first try."

The controversial ruling occurred with seven and a half minutes remaining in regulation and North Carolina holding a 20-15 lead. South Carolina rallied to tie the score at 28-28 and send the game into overtime. Each team scored two points and a second overtime was necessary with the score tied at 30-30.

Bennie Tompkins converted a free throw and Ed Nevergold a field goal in the first two minutes of the second overtime to put the Gamecocks up 33-30. Wilmer Hines of North Carolina made a long shot to cut the margin to one point, but Bennie Tompkins was fouled as the overtime ended and made the free throw after time had elapsed to put South Carolina in the championship game against Duke.

Duke reached the championship game by defeating Virginia 38-24 and Washington & Lee 41-32.

The Gamecocks made page one in *The State* with a banner headline that said: "Carolina Wins Southern Conference Basketball Championship."

Two sub-heads added, "Gamecocks Lick Duke at Raleigh," and "Come From Behind to Capture Championship."

The Associated Press, in its game story, said, "South Carolina's high powered Gamecocks whipped Duke 33 to 21, here tonight for the Southern Conference basketball championship.

"The Blue Devils, who were making their third appearance in the finals of the annual basketball tournament, outscored the Gamecocks 15-13 in the first half, but couldn't keep up the pace after the intermission and South Carolina pulled away to a safe lead.."

Both Tompkins brothers made the All Southern Conference first team selected at the tournament and Dana Henderson was on the second team. A year later Freddie Tompkins would be named to the Chuck Taylor Converse Yearbook All America team.

Freddie Tompkins and Henderson scored 13 points each in the championship game and the AP said the Gamecocks "were just too tall for the Blue Devils." The wire story noted the South Carolina team "includes four sophomores who were members of the Athens (Tex.) high school team which won national honors."

Freddie Tompkins was an All-America player on great South Carolina teams of 1933 and '34.
—USC Sports Information

Three Gamecocks—both Tompkins brothers and Henderson—were six feet four inches tall, John Rowland was described as "a fraction of an inch under six feet," and Vic Laurie, a starter until Freddie Tompkins and Wolf became eligible and a key reserve after that, was six feet two.

Bennie Tompkins scored four points in the championship game and Rowland scored the other three. Wolf, the fifth starter, and Laurie, the only substitute, did not score.

Caldwell Withers, writing in *The Columbia Record*, said, "overpowering second half strength coupled with a decline in their opponents stamina and an unerring aim for the basket brought the Southern Conference basketball championship to the University of South Carolina."

Withers added the Gamecocks had a shaky start, trailing Duke 15-8 in the first half, but "came forward rapidly in the second half and ran away with the game."

The State reported its telephones "rang incessantly," and the large crowds around the newspaper's bulletin board "reminded one of football season."

After the game, the South Carolina team rushed to the Raleigh railroad station and boarded an 11:55 p. m., train, changing trains in Charlotte and arriving at the Columbia station at 7:45 a. m.

After beginning the season with a 2-2 road trip, South Carolina won its final 15 games to finish with a 17-2 record and the Southern Conference championship.

An Associated Press story, distributed nationwide and published by *The State* February 12, 1933 featured the four players from Texas. The four sophomores so dominated the 1933 Gamecock team that the veterans played only in backup roles. Team captain J. L. "Buck" Smith scored 12 points during the entire season.

Kentucky, the last team to defeat the Gamecocks before their run to the championship and South Carolina's victim in Freddie Tompkins' first game, meanwhile, was winning the first Southeastern Conference tournament in Atlanta under Coach Adolph Rupp. The Wildcats had reached the finals seven times in their last nine Southern Conference tournaments but had never won the title as Vanderbilt was the dominant team in those years.

After one season, Laval returned South Carolina's head coaching duties to Rock Norman and the winning streak stretched to a school record 32 as the Gamecocks won their first 17 games of 1934.

An outbreak of mumps weakened the squad, however, and South Carolina was upset by N. C. State, 43-24, in the opening round of the 1934 Southern Conference tournament at Raleigh. South Carolina defeated Pittsburgh 38-35 in a home game played after the tournament to finish 1934 with an 18-1 mark.

Financial problems in the athletic program resulted in cuts in scholarship aid and the Tompkins brothers did not play their senior season and the 1935 record was 15-9, including a first round, 46-25, loss to North Carolina in the conference tournament.

Freddie Tompkins, inducted as a charter member of the University of South Carolina Athletic Hall of Fame in 1967, actually played only 32 games for the Gamecocks, 13 in a partial season, 1934, and 19 in 1935.

He averaged 14.1 points per game each season and with him in the lineup, South Carolina's record was 31-1.

11

South Carolina

vs

Duke

March 7, 1957---South Carolina 84, Duke 81
(Atlantic Coast Conference Tournament)

at Raleigh, N. C.

The high scoring exploits of South Carolina forward Grady Wallace during the 1957 basketball season put him on a first name basis with *The State*, Columbia's morning newspaper.

More and more, in headlines and in the body of game stories and features, the paper referred to him as "Grady" than by his last name.

"The great Grady, leading the nation in scoring..."

"Grady Leads USC to Stunning Upset..."

"Gangling Grady," etc.

The slim, six foot four inch (some rosters listed him as 6-5), 175 pound senior from the little hamlet of Mare Creek, Kentucky captured the hearts of journalists as well as all Gamecock fans as he marched toward the NCAA Division I scoring championship.

In 29 games, Wallace scored 906 points for an average of 31.25 points per game to win a five way battle for the scoring title over Joe Gibbon of Mississippi, Elgin Baylor of Seattle, Wilt Chamberlain of Kansas and Chet Forte of Columbia, all of whom averaged between 28.9 and 30.05 points per game.

After two years at Pikeville Junior College in Kentucky, Wallace enrolled at South Carolina in the fall of 1955 for his junior and senior seasons. He averaged 23.9, scoring 550 points as a junior before soaring to the national title as a senior.

His two season career average was 28.0 on 1,456 points in 52 games as a Gamecock.

In leading South Carolina to a 17-12 record in 1957, Wallace led his team in scoring in 22 of 29 games. He scored fewer than 20 points only twice, 16 in a 75-61 win over N.C. State at Charlotte, and 11 in a 75-62 loss to eventual NCAA champion North Carolina at

Chapel Hill, a game in which South Carolina led by two points at halftime.

To demonstrate his versatility, Wallace also led the Atlantic Coast Conference in rebounding with an average of 14.4 per game.

Seven times Wallace scored in the 30s and six times in the 40s, with his top effort coming on the road, 54 points in a 96-81 win over Georgia December 21, 1956 in Athens. That remained a school single game record until John Roche scored 56 points February 4, 1971 in a 118-83 win over Furman at Columbia.

Wallace, as of 1995, still held the second, third, fourth and fifth best single game total with 45 points against N. C. State at Raleigh, and 44 twice, against Virginia and Clemson at Columbia in 1957. He also scored 43 against The Citadel at home and Duke on the road.

Grady Wallace averaged 31.3 points per game to lead the nation in scoring in 1957.—*USC Sports Information*

However, perhaps the greatest performance by Wallace occurred at Raleigh March 7, 1957 in the opening round of the Atlantic Coast Conference Tournament when he scored 41 points, including the final 14 by his team in one of the greatest comebacks in Gamecock history.

South Carolina, with a 15-11 regular season record, was seeded sixth and hadn't advanced beyond the first game in post season play since 1947 when the Gamecocks were in the Southern Conference. Ironically, South Carolina beat Duke 56-54 in the first round that year.

Duke was seeded third in the 1957 ACC tournament and the Blue Devils were prohibitive favorites over the Gamecocks, having easily won both regular season meetings, 104-76 at Columbia in December and 94-81 at Durham in February despite Wallace's 43 point effort.

Frank McGuire, coach of undefeated and top-seeded North Carolina, felt Duke would make the tournament finals, calling the Blue Devils "a very powerful team."

South Carolina coach Frank Johnson said he would "rather play most any team in the conference than Duke" in the 2 p. m., game that opened the tournament on Thursday, March 7.

The Associated Press announced its All-America team a couple of days before the ACC tournament and *The State* showed its disappointment with this headline: "AP Fails to Select Wallace on First Team All America."

The Gamecock ace and eventual NCAA scoring champion made the AP's second team. He was a first team choice by United Press, International News Service, Helm's Athletic Foundation, and Chuck Taylor's Converse Yearbook, however.

Things did not start out well for the underdog Gamecocks. Duke led 28-14 after ten minutes and Wallace didn't score his first field goal until there was 8:06 remaining in the half.

"In the beginning they had a bad case of their chronic malady —tournament jitters," Bill Rone wrote in *The State*. They made every mistake in the book."

Wallace began to warm up and Rone said, "with their leader back on the beam, the Gamecocks began to move. It wasn't a dramatic change, but rather a gradual, on again, off again, advance that gradually cut into Duke's margin."

Suddenly, the Gamecocks erupted with four consecutive baskets, "including two one handers by Grady and quickly cut Duke's lead to 38-35."

Bucky Allen's field goal gave Duke a five point halftime lead, 40-35. Wallace had 14 points at intermission.

Ray "Cookie" Pericola made two driving layups and was fouled, converting both three point plays, and suddenly the upstart Gamecocks led, 48-46, early in the second half. South Carolina led 52-50 before Duke rattled off nine consecutive points and, in Rone's words, "it appeared all over but the shouting."

The Gamecock cause looked even more hopeless when six foot eight inch Fred Lentz, a key rebounder, fouled out with 5:17 left to play. Lentz's departure "left an ominous note," Rone wrote.

However, he added, "Wallace was moving into one of the greatest five minutes of his sparkling career."

Duke's lead was 79-72 when Wallace scored from the side to raise his personal total to 31 points and cut the Blue Devil lead to 5.

"The Blue Devils began to slow it down, playing for the layup. It was in the bag, but the bag had a hole in it. They couldn't hit the layups or make the free throws," was the way Rone described it.

Wallace scored from underneath, added two free throws, and with 20 seconds left in the game, he drove to the basket for a layup to tie the score and was fouled. His free throw made the score 82-81, Carolina.

Richie Hoffman grabbed a key rebound off a Duke miss and passed off to Wallace who was fouled. With five seconds remaining, Grady sank two free throws and the game was over—South Carolina 84, Duke 81.

Grady Wallace scored South Carolina's last 14 points and finished with 41. Wallace sank 13 field goals and made 15 of 17 free throw attempts as the Gamecocks as a team made 26 of 30 from the foul line. Duke was eliminated in the first round for the first time.

Bill Rone, in a sidebar story, declared, "If a team can be sloppy and magnificent at the same time, that is what South Carolina's Gamecocks were. They were rather pathetic in the first ten minutes...They goofed easy shots, threw the ball away and couldn't buy an offensive rebound...They finally shook their jitters but were never a polished club until the end."

In a post game interview, Wallace said "the difference between today's game and the ones we lost to Duke during the season? Well, they ran us to death before. Today we didn't let them."

Coach Frank Johnson was amazed by his team's comeback.

"I didn't know whether we could win it or not when we fell 14 points behind in the first half," he said. "But you've got to give these kids credit. They never gave up."

Although Wallace was the obvious hero, Johnson singled out the Gamecock defense down the stretch.

"If I had to put my finger on one factor that won for us," he said, "I would say our defense in the last five minutes and the fact that we didn't have to foul too much to get the ball."

Assistant coach Walt Hambrick thought three sophomores, Cookie Pericola, Richie Hoffman and Fred Lentz, were also instrumental in the victory. Pericola scored 16 points and directed the attack from his guard position, Hoffman scored 10 and got two key rebounds, and Lentz was a key rebounder and contributed 10 points.

Frank Johnson coached NCAA scoring champion Grady Wallace during his 15 seasons as head coach.—*USC Sports Information*

Duke coach Hal Bradley blamed the defeat more on his team's failure to execute than on South Carolina's performance.

"We missed the layups and free throws that could have iced the game for us," Bradley said. "That, and that alone beat us. I don't ever recall blowing that big a lead late in a game."

Bradley said he changed defensive strategy on Wallace from two regular season meetings, both won by Duke, when Wallace scored 21 and 43 points.

"We played him tight but let it sag a bit. We had one man on him but dropped off a guard or a center to keep him inside," Bradley explained.

The Duke coach paid grudging tribute to the South Carolina All-America, saying "he's good but I still think (Lennie) Rosenbluth (of North Carolina) is the better offensive man."

After the triumph over Duke, the Gamecocks upset second seeded Maryland, 74-64 behind Wallace's 31 points and 17 rebounds by Fred Lentz to reach the championship game against North Carolina, which remained undefeated after beating Clemson 81-61 and eking out a 61-59 squeaker over Wake Forest in the semi-finals.

In two regular season games South Carolina took the Tar Heels into overtime at Columbia before losing 90-86, and led 40-38 at halftime before dropping a 75-62 decision at Chapel Hill. Wallace scored 35 points against the Tar Heels in Columbia but was held to a season low 11 points in the game at Chapel Hill.

The third time around, in the ACC tournament championship game, Wallace scored 28 points but the Tar Heels prevailed 95-75 and went on to win two triple overtime games in the NCAA Tournament, over Michigan State and over Kansas for the national championship.

Wallace and North Carolina's Rosenbluth were unanimous picks for the all-tournament team selected by the news media. Others on the first team were Jackie Murdock and Jack Williams of Wake Forest and Pete Brennan of North Carolina.

Seven years later Frank McGuire, who led North Carolina to that NCAA title, would begin a sixteen year tenure as South Carolina's head basketball coach.

Grady Wallace played a year with the Phillips Oilers AAU team and eventually returned to South Carolina where he became executive director of the state probation, pardon and parole board.

III

South Carolina

vs

Western Kentucky

December 27, 1963--South Carolina 75, Western Kentucky 60

at Nashville, Tennessee

The Chuck Noe coached basketball teams at the University of South Carolina between 1962 and 1964 were fun to watch.

They didn't win many games. Noe's record in a season and a half was 15-21 before a near nervous breakdown forced him out of the coaching profession for several years. Noe never had much in the way of size, depth, and the other necessities to produce a consistent winner, but his teams were scrappy and the feisty little coach had a creative mind that consistently came up with innovations that kept a lot of games close.

Not all of his tactics involved strategy on the court. Noe stationed the pep band behind the visitor's bench in the old Carolina Field House. Duke coach Vic Bubas countered by taking his team to mid-court for consultation during times out. Those on the bench had to duck the slide trombones.

Sports editor Jake Penland of *The State*, Columbia's morning newspaper, called Noe a "bantam rooster."

Noe came to South Carolina in the spring of 1962 after some success at Virginia Tech. He had been voted Southern Conference Coach of the Year after the 1961-62 season. Bob Stevens had departed for Oklahoma after a 15-12 season that earned him Atlantic Coast Conference Coach of the Year honors.

However, five of the top eight players from that Gamecock squad were gone and Noe found the cupboard nearly bare.

His first South Carolina team won only nine of twenty four games. His tallest starter was six foot four inch senior Bob Haney who had a bad back but managed to average 8.3 points per game. The stars were 6-1 senior Scotti Ward, 17.6 points per game, and 6-3 junior Ronnie Collins, 16.6. Two other juniors, 6-1 Jimmy Collins, no relation to Ronnie, and 6-3 Bill Yarborough, averaged 9.8 and 7.5 points per game, respectively.

This under sized iron man crew, with very little help from the bench, other than 6-0 junior Terry Lucansky, battled North Carolina down to the wire in the 1963 North-South doubleheaders, then played in the Charlotte Coliseum, before losing by four points, 78-74. The following night, in two overtimes, Noe's Gamecocks upset North Carolina State 70-68.

An incident during halftime of the January 29, 1963 game with Duke involved the Price family and caused much embarrassment for my wife, Margaret. Fans were asked to throw March of Dimes contributions on the court during halftime. Cheerleaders, aided by a number of youngsters from the stands, scooped up the coins.

The three Price youngsters—Tommy, 11, Melissa, 8, and Richard, 7—joined the proceedings. The only problem was, Richard didn't understand about charity. He thought it was free money. When a cheerleader asked for his collections, his reaction was, "No way!"

His older brother grabbed him, kicking and screaming, turned him upside down, and coins tumbled out of his bulging pockets and were properly directed to the March of Dimes.

Margaret was mortified and the overflow crowd in the 3,200 capacity field house roared.

Haney and Ward were gone when pre-season practice began for the 1963-64 season but 6-6 sophomore John Schroeder was up from the freshman team and Lucansky moved into the starting lineup with the two Collins boys and Yarborough.

Schroeder was a non-scorer. Teammates nicknamed him "Ice Man" because they said he always had a cold shooting hand. However, he was a team leader, a tireless defensive player, and contributed much while averaging 4.4 points per game in the 69 games he played over three seasons.

In the season opening game, at Chapel Hill, South Carolina again took the Tar Heels to the wire before falling by five, 92-87. The Gamecocks led by 19 points before Billy Cunningham, who scored 25, sparked a Tar Heel comeback.

Always an admirer of superior talent, Noe made his way to the North Carolina locker room after the game to shake Cunningham's hand.

"I love that Cunningham," Noe told reporters. "When things get tight, his eyes get big and he turns it on."

About his own team, Noe said, "I don't believe in moral victories but I'm proud of these kids of mine. They won't quit."

Noe vowed to come up with something to give his scrawny little band a fighting chance. The Mongoose offense was born.

Although only six feet three, 160 pounds, Ronnie Collins of Winnsboro, S. C., was a star scorer and rebounder for the Gamecocks, 1962-64. Here he is fouled by Russ Marvel of N. C. State.—*Tom Price Files*

Noe stationed 6-3 Ronnie Collins along the base line in the left corner with 6-1 Jimmy Collins opposite in the right corner. Terry Lucansky set up on the left side out near the mid-court line with 6-3 Bill Yarborough on the right side and 6-6 John Schroeder in the middle near the center circle.

There was no shot clock rule in effect and the Gamecocks would hold the basketball with Lucansky occasionally passing it back and forth to Schroeder or Yarborough. If the opponents were lulled to sleep or became impatient and attempted to take the ball away, Ronnie would break to the basket for a layup, Yarborough would drive to the basket, or the ball would go to Jimmy for a jump shot.

It was a stall offense that often produced points.

Noe sprang the Mongoose on Georgia in the old Carolina Field House and startled the Bulldogs as the Gamecocks took a 17 point victory, 77-60.

Beat writer Jeff Denberg's story in *The State* stated Georgia became confused by the Gamecock back court passing the ball back and forth out by the time line.

"Georgia, confused, stood its ground," Denberg wrote. "Time passed—Finally, Georgia came out to get the Gamecocks. Then, the Mongoose sprang. Yarborough passed to Ronnie. He hit from six feet away. It was the first shot of the game and the "Cocks led 2-0 after 2 minutes and 4 seconds. Georgia got its first field goal with 7 minutes left in the half."

Ronnie Collins scored 13 field goals and made 11 of 12 free throw attempts and his 37 points accounted for nearly half of South Carolina's total. Yarborough scored 21, Jimmy Collins 11, with the remainder of the Gamecocks—Lucansky, Schroeder and Jim Fox, a 6-10 junior college addition—combining for 7 points.

"Brains, guts and discipline were the keys," according to Denberg. "Chuck Noe supplied the brains, his kids the guts. They combined for the discipline."

In a post game interview, Noe said, "The way to beat Georgia was to keep the ball away from them. I saw they had some impatient boys on their team and I knew they were deeper than us. They have more good players than we have. If we had run with them we wouldn't have had a chance."

Three days after the win over Georgia, Coach Lyles Alley brought his Furman team to Columbia and showed more patience against Noe's Mongoose offense, but the result was the same although the scoring was much lower.

Ronnie Collins scored 17 points in the first half, the remainder of the Gamecocks combined for 2, and South Carolina held a 19-17 lead. Ronnie finished with 30, the rest of the team had 15, and the final score was 45-32.

Coach Alley said of South Carolina, "They played their kind of basketball as perfectly as it could be played."

Denberg credited "passes from John Schroeder and Bill Yarborough, help from Jimmy Collins and the ghostly Bill Yarborough" for setting Ronnie up to score two-thirds of the Gamecock total, as well as a Furman zone defense "that all but ignored Ronnie."

Noe credited "poise" by his iron five.

South Carolina next battled Duke down to the wire but lost 77-70, and went winless on a trip to the Blue Grass state, losing to Kentucky Wesleyan and Louisville. After a brief break for Christmas, the 2-4 Gamecocks reassembled in Nashville for the Vanderbilt Invitational Tournament, meeting Western Kentucky in the opening round while Vanderbilt took on Memphis State.

Veteran Western Kentucky coach Eddie Diddle brought a 754-286 career record to Nashville. Only Phog Allen of Kansas, with 771 victories, had won more games. But Diddle wasn't happy that his team was coming off a nine day holiday layoff.

"Too much Christmas," he fretted.

The Gamecocks kept it close, trailing by a point at halftime, and took the lead early in the second half. The Mongoose came into play.

When South Carolina went into the spread offense, Western Kentucky laid back. The rules required the defensive team to come out and play if it was behind or the score was tied. After thirty seconds of stall, the officials motioned to the Hilltoppers to come out and pressure the ball.

Diddle signaled his defenders to stay back. Five seconds after the warning, a technical foul was whistled on Western Kentucky.

Mr. Diddle's red towel—his long time trade mark—went sailing into the air and his shrill voice could be heard screaming, "What?"

From that point on, psychology was on the side of Chuck Noe and the Gamecocks. South Carolina won going away, 75-60.

"South Carolina's Gamecocks came from a point down at the half with the Mongoose offense and broke a three game losing streak as they handed Western Kentucky a 75-60 defeat and gained the finals of the Vanderbilt Invitational Tournament," Jeff Denberg wrote in *The State.*"

"The Gamecocks completely dominated the second half, holding the Hilltoppers to 9 field goals and 6 points from the foul line," Denberg added.

Ronnie Collins scored 24 points and the 6-3, 160 pound forward also cornered 12 rebounds. Bill Yarborough scored 21 with his driving layups and claimed 14 rebounds, despite battling a case of influenza. Jimmy Collins scored 10 points and Jim Fox came off the bench to pull down 8 rebounds, and added 6 points.

Bane Sarratt kept Western Kentucky within striking distance with 23 points, scored mostly on base line jumpers from the corner.

"South Carolina won despite shooting only 41.7 per cent on field goals and making 15 of 29 free throws," Denberg noted. "But, what Coach Chuck Noe's team did do was hustle. They stayed after Western in the first half even after falling behind by 10 points, 28-18. From that point, the Gamecocks outscored Western 52-32.

The Gamecocks went into their 3-2, or Mongoose, attack whenever they were tied or ahead and it worked perfectly. The Kentuckians grew over anxious and the Birds were able to set up Ronnie and Yarborough for layups."

Denberg said South Carolina made up for its miscues with "a hustling, nose to nose, defense that forced Western turnovers."

Chuck Noe told his team it was, "A heck of a win. Bless your hearts."

He told the news media, "When kids play like they do and never give up, something's got to fall. We went behind and came back. Yarborough was sick and he played a great game. Fox played his best game."

Host team Vanderbilt, ranked sixth nationally under coach Roy Skinner, defeated Memphis State, 85-79, to remain unbeaten and join South Carolina the following night in the championship game.

Skinner, incidentally, had a South Carolina background. He was a graduate of Presbyterian College at Clinton where he was an infielder on the baseball team.

His Commodores were led by 6-9 twin towers Clyde Lee and Bob "Snake" Grace, and a perpetual motion little guard named John Ed Miller.

On paper, South Carolina was far outmanned by the talented Commodores, but that didn't prevent Chuck Noe from sitting up all night trying to come up with a victory plan. At 3 a. m., there was a knock on the door to my room in the Andrew Jackson Hotel. It was Chuck Noe.

"Help me figure out a way to beat Vanderbilt," the Bantam Rooster coach pleaded as he scratched out X's and O's on a hotel note pad. "There's got to be a way."

Needless to say, I wasn't much help.

The Columbia Record, in its pre-game story, said, "South Carolina's patient but prudent Gamecocks are cast in the role of giant killers tonight against unbeaten and nationally ranked Vanderbilt for the championship of the Vanderbilt Invitational Tournament."

Alas, it was not to be. Fatigue and Bill Yarborough's 'flu bug, and Vanderbilt's superior talent were just too much. South Carolina was within striking distance, trailing by only 10 points, 57-47, when Yarborough fouled out with 12 minutes and 18 seconds left in the game. The roof fell in on the Gamecocks after that.

The Mongoose offense and the innovative mind of Chuck Noe were no match for the tall and talented Commodores on their home court and Vanderbilt won easily, 106-78, despite a 35 point effort from Ronnie Collins. His 59 points in two games earned him a spot on the all-tournament team.

The already painfully depth shy Gamecocks suffered a crippling blow when Jim Fox, who had joined the team as a junior following two junior college seasons, was ruled academically ineligible for the second semester.

Chuck Noe would coach only four more games with the Gamecocks, winning three of them, before winding up in a hospital for treatment of mental exhaustion. He defeated Virginia 70-62 and Maryland 73-69 in overtime in the first two games of a road trip, but lost to Georgia Tech in Atlanta, 87-73, before ending his career with a 51-44 Mongoose dominated win over North Carolina State in the Carolina Field House.

Furman Bisher, sports editor of the Atlanta *Journal*, wrote a column when Noe's team visited Georgia Tech, likening the Gamecocks to a circus "with their own giant and midget," referring to six foot ten inch center Jim Fox and three foot eight inch trainer Johnny Downs who was a dwarf.

It became evident in the game at Maryland that Noe was ill. When the regulation game ended in a tie, Noe appeared convinced the Gamecocks had won, and he rushed over to the Maryland bench to shake Terrapin Coach Bud Milliken's hand.

Assistant Coach Dwane Morrison gently guided Noe back to the South Carolina bench and convinced him the game was going into overtime. Noe, who often drew plays on the floor with chalk to put across a point during times out, regained his composure, was his usual brilliant self during the five minute overtime and the Gamecocks prevailed by four points.

Noe left the 1963-64 Gamecocks with a 6-6 record. Morrison was the only full time assistant coach and he became the interim head coach, assisted only by graduate assistant Bob Haney, and the Gamecocks won four games and lost eight the remainder of the season to finish with a 10-14 record.

Noe remained out of coaching for a time and then worked as a volunteer assistant to Coach Vic Bubas at Duke before becoming

Terry Lucansky earned a Ph.D. and became a professor and department head at the University of Florida.—*USC Sports Information*

head coach at Virginia Commonwealth University in Richmond. For many years after that he hosted a talk show on a Richmond radio station.

Some years later, North Carolina's Dean Smith used elements of Noe's Mongoose offense, but moved the center from near midcourt to a spot near the free throw line and called it the "four corners."

Ronnie Collins became an executive with Duke Power Co., in North Carolina. Jimmy Collins became a radio station general manager in Columbia. John Schroeder went to work for IBM. Terry Lucansky went to graduate school, earned a Ph.D., and became a professor and department head at the University of Florida. Bill Yarborough went to medical school and set up a practice in Honolulu, Hawaii.

Jim Fox regained his eligibility as a senior and was the leading scorer, averaging 17.8 points per game, on the first Frank McGuire coached team at South Carolina—a team that won only six games.

After two years in the European basketball league, Fox had a ten year career in the National Basketball Association.

After retiring from the NBA, he owned a deep sea charter fishing boat in Georgia and became a contractor specializing in the construction of tennis courts in Phoenix, Ariz.

IV

South Carolina

vs

Duke

December 6, 1965--South Carolina 73, Duke 71

at Columbia

Executive Sports Editor Herman Helms of *The State*, Columbia's morning newspaper, called it "the biggest basketball victory in USC history," and well it might have been.

It was the first of many major wins over nationally ranked opponents during Frank McGuire's sixteen seasons as the University of South Carolina's head basketball coach.

It vaulted the Gamecocks into a spot among the nation's top ten, and while they didn't stay there very long that season, it set the stage for a string of national rankings in the years that followed.

It ignited basketball fever throughout the Palmetto State and hurried along the construction of new basketball facilities for the Gamecocks and their chief instate rival, Clemson.

In short, South Carolina's 73-71 upset of nationally third ranked Duke in the old Carolina Field House on December 6, 1965, revolutionized college basketball in the state of South Carolina.

The Gamecocks had a national scoring champion and an All-America in the person of Grady Wallace in 1957, and had great teams featuring the Tompkins brothers in 1933 and 1934. Furman had had several All America players and national scoring champions in Frank Selvy and Darrell Floyd. Clemson had had a two sport All America in Banks McFadden in the 1930s.

But, for sheer impact on one school's program and collegiate basketball in an entire state, the shocking win over Duke in the third game of the 1965-66 season, was unequaled.

Duke, under Coach Vic Bubas, had gone to the NCAA championship game the previous March before losing to UCLA, and was a heavy favorite to repeat as Atlantic Coast Conference champion.

In his pre-season assessment of the ACC race, Jeff Denberg, basketball beat writer for *The State*, wrote: "For years the going cliché in the Atlantic Coast Conference went like this: Duke is so good Vic Bubas could divide his squad and both teams would finish in the top ten.."

In fact, one published pre-season poll, through typographic error, ranked the Blue Devils fifth and seventh, prompting North Carolina State Coach Press Maravich to quip, "See, this is the first team," pointing to the fifth spot, "and this is the second team" in the seventh position.

Denberg said reasons for Duke's lofty position included such veteran star players as Steve Vacendak, Bob Verga, Jack Marin and Bob Reidy, and "a healthy six foot seven inch plus, 220 pound sophomore named Mike Lewis."

Denberg's assessment was five ACC teams might give Duke a good fight but "Virginia and South Carolina are on another plateau—considerably lower."

"If anyone is going to beat Duke," Denberg asserted, "the logical choice is Maryland." The Terps boasted such star names as Jay McMillen, Gary Ward, Joe Harrington, Rick Wise, Neil Brayton and Gary Williams.

South Carolina, coming off a 6-17 record in Frank McGuire's first season, was without 6-7, 235 pound scorer-rebounder Gary Gregor, ruled ineligible in mid-season the year before, and 6-9 center Jim Fox, off to Europe for two years before beginning a National Basketball Association career that spanned ten seasons.

Fox had averaged 17.8 points and 13.6 rebounds per game as a senior and Gregor contributed a 16.7 point average in six December games. Also gone was guard Jerry Croke, who averaged 14.2. Returning starters included 6-9 junior Al Salvadori, 11.0, and guard Earl Lovelace, 9.6.

John Schroeder, a 6-6, blue collar type of player who couldn't jump or shoot but was a tenacious defensive player and a fierce competitor, was a contributing senior. Lyn Burkholder, a 6-10 junior with massive hands, was another hard worker with limited scoring potential.

Gamecock hopes, however, hinged on four sophomore imports from New York and New Jersey who had been the mainstays of the 1964-65 freshman team. Guards Jack Thompson of The Bronx and Skip Harlicka of Trenton, N. J., forward Frank Standard of Brooklyn and center Skip Kickey of Union City, N. J., were the first of McGuire's "underground railroad" recruits from up east.

Harlicka had led the freshman team with a 24.1 average and Standard had averaged 20.9. Kickey and Thompson both scored in double figures and Thompson dazzled those who came early to watch the freshman games with his passing skills until sidelined by an ankle injury in the second half of the season.

Jeff Denberg wrote there were two ways to look at South Carolina's 1965-66 basketball prospects:

1. In comparison to the big shots of the Atlantic Coast Conference, it may not be much of a team at all.

2. In comparison to what they were last year, the Gamecocks will be a delight to behold.

McGuire looked upon his second season as a building year, saying "unless you have a group of super stars, you won't win with sophomores," adding, "sophomores should spend their time learning from the juniors and seniors."

Denberg felt that Standard, a 6-4, 190 pound craggy faced base line player, "who resembles a young Abe Lincoln, may turn out to be the surprise of the team."

Denberg's final assessment on the Gamecock team before the season opener was, "it will almost certainly finish in the second division (of the ACC), but it will not be beaten badly after a time. It will have a chance to defend itself and, perhaps, knock off a few of the big clubs."

The Gamecocks opened the season with a 66-52 win over little Erskine College with four players scoring in double figures, led by Salvadori's 18 points and Standard's 17 rebounds. Salvadori, who had replaced his thick, horn rimmed, glasses with contact lenses, said "I could see better. I felt free out there."

In a road game, at Furman, South Carolina battered the Paladins 97-79 with Harlicka scoring 23 points, Salvadori 22, Standard 17 and Thompson 16, on the same night that Duke, displaying "awesome mastery" in the opinion of writer Add Penfield, Jr., of *The State*, outrebounded Clemson 53-23 in an 83-68 win at Durham.

Duke was ranked number three in the nation when the Blue Devils arrived in Columbia for a Monday night game. Most of the talk was about the Blue Devils' rematch in Durham the following Saturday with defending national champion UCLA. The South Carolina media looked upon that game as a homecoming for UCLA guard Kenny Washington of Beaufort, S. C., who had scored 24 points off the bench against Duke in the NCAA title game.

Duke Coach Vic Bubas predicted his Blue Devils "will have to be at our best against South Carolina. Its always been that way when we have played here. We expect South Carolina to hold the ball and let the air out a bit. We'll probably have to go out and get it from them."

The Gamecocks didn't hold the ball, however. They didn't try to run with Duke either. They played it straight up, patiently, but didn't stall, capitalizing on the ball handling and passing skills of Thompson to control tempo and take a 38-37 halftime lead. The Gamecocks had played the Blue Devils within two points, 62-60, in the opening round of the 1965 ACC tournament, and perhaps there was a carry-over confidence that they could play with the big boys, although most of the South Carolina players from that team were either gone or relegated to bench duty.

The Gamecocks were called for 12 personal fouls in the first 13 minutes of the second half and trailed by as many as six points but battled back to tie the score at 56-56 with 11:40 to play, only to undergo a three and a half minute scoring drought that put Duke again ahead by six, 62-56.

Officials called two technical fouls, one on McGuire and one on Buck Freeman, the first technical the veteran Gamecock assistant had received in more than forty years. Freeman said after the game he was "embarrassed."

Standard's tip in cut Duke's lead to 67-64 with 4:09 remaining. Harlicka's 15 foot jump shot cut it to 1 at 69-68 with the clock showing 2:55.

Now, it was Duke that went into a stall. The Blue Devils spread the floor and played keep away, hoping the Gamecocks would foul or leave a Blue Devil open for a layup. Jack Marin took a shot with a minute and a half to play and it missed. Al Salvadori rebounded for the Gamecocks and put the ball in the hands of Jack Thompson.

His thread needle pass found Salvadori breaking from the left corner to the basket and he scored and was hacked across the arm by Bob Reidy. Sal, as his teammates called him sank the free throw and suddenly the upstart Gamecocks had a two point lead, 71-69, with less than a minute remaining.

The 3,500 who jammed the 3,200 capacity, 39 year old Carolina Field House, were in a frenzy.

With 34 seconds left Vacendak worked free and scored from 10 feet to tie it at 71-71.

Thompson dribbled slowly upcourt, spotted Standard breaking from right to left along the baseline, and whipped him a pass that Standard laid in the basketball to again give South Carolina a two point lead. Duke, however, had 20 seconds to do something about that.

Reidy missed a jump shot. Lewis and Marin missed tips, and Standard, diving through the air, tipped the loose ball out to Harlicka and tumbled to the floor.

"I slapped at it," Standard recalled in the locker room after the game. "I remember knocking it out and falling down. Then I looked up at the clock and it said one second. I knew Skippy had the ball

Jack Thompson was a superb playmaking guard, 1966-68.—*USC Sports Information*

and I thought Oh, God! We got a winner. A winner! Then I rolled over."

South Carolina had beaten third ranked Duke 73-71. It was the first Gamecock win over the Blue Devils since a Grady Wallace led, 84-81, win in the 1957 ACC tournament at Raleigh.

Harlicka scored 19 points, Standard and Thompson had 17 each, and Salvadori scored 12. Thompson had nine assists.

The State ran a banner headline across its first sports page heralding: "Standard's Basket With 0:20 Left Guns USC to Startling Upset of Duke, 73-71."

Jeff Denberg's game story led: "South Carolina's passing magician Jack Thompson hit Frank Standard with a perfect pass which Standard took into the nets 20 seconds from the end Monday night to give South Carolina a fairy tale, 73-71, victory over third ranked Duke in a field house that broke into sheer frenzy.

"The Gamecocks, figured to finish no better than seventh in the Atlantic Coast Conference and seemingly down after a spunky effort with nine minutes to play, came back the way Duke is supposed to, finally making up a six point deficit with 52 seconds left when Al Salvadori took another of Thompson's press-shredding passes and went high to make it 70-69.

"Salvadori, who was hacked on the arm by Duke's Bob Reidy on the way up, put his free throw in the basket..."

The crowd, most of them students, surged onto the floor and hoisted McGuire and Thompson to their shoulders, giving both a pummeling in the process.

In the visitor's locker room, Vic Bubas thought South Carolina's guards—sophomores Thompson and Harlicka—were the difference in the game.

"The offensive work of those guards was nothing short of phenomenal," he said. "I don't know if in the course of conference play we'll run across guard play that good or not. They're going to be tough to handle. We couldn't handle it tonight."

Lewis, who led the Blue Devil rebounding, said "this was by far the toughest game under the boards we have had this year."

"That's one of the worst physical beatings I've had, when they put me up on their shoulders," McGuire said after he finally made it to the locker room. "But, it's one I enjoyed."

McGuire, who had won an NCAA championship as coach at North Carolina in 1957, called the win over Duke "one of the greatest."

"They didn't give up when they were behind," he said of his Gamecocks. "They didn't get frantic."

The coach said the Gamecocks might have been better off slowing the tempo to a near stall, "but here, before the home crowd, we'll just play the game."

McGuire said Duke was playing Thompson for the jump shot on the winning play, "so we tried to go inside. We had three plays ready to go. I thought Thompson was going to take the shot, but he passed off. He fooled me all right. These kids are gifted, You never know what they're going to do."

The Gamecock coach called Duke explosive, and said "if you try to run with them, then you go right out the window."

Herman Helms, in a follow up column in *The State*, wrote:

"There are secrets behind extraordinary men like Frank McGuire, who stand at the top of their professions. No one had anticipated that he would bring Carolina this big a win so soon."

Jeff Denberg, in a sidebar story, paid tribute to blue collar worker John Schroeder, bumped from the spotlight by more talented players. Denberg called Schroeder—nicknamed "Ice Man" because he had cold shooting hands, "was the glue that held the team together."

All five Duke starters scored in double figures in the game, led by Lewis with 17. Verga scored 15, Marin 13, Reidy 12 and Vacendak 11, but the Duke bench contributed only 3 points. The Blue Devils out rebounded the Gamecocks 49-33 and made 19 of 28 free throws to South Carolina's 11 of 21. However, the Gamecocks made 31 of 57 field goal attempts, 54 per cent, to Duke's 26 of 63, 41 per cent.

The big victory rocketed South Carolina to 10th place in the Associated Press poll, their first time among the nation's top ten, and Duke dropped to sixth.

There was disturbing news in the sports world that week. Baseball mogul Branch Rickey died at the age of 83, Virginia Tech's bid to become the ninth member of the Atlantic Coast Conference was rejected, and both South Carolina and Clemson were fined $2,500 for being over the ACCs newly imposed limit of 140 football scholarships.

However, the sun shone brightly on the Gamecock basketball program.

The following weekend in Durham, Duke—whose 115 wins over the past five seasons were the most by any team in the country—trounced defending NCAA champion UCLA, 82-66.

South Carolina rode its 3-0 record and top ten ranking to Philadelphia where the Gamecocks, using the slow down tactics that Vic Bubas had expected on Monday night, defeated 15th ranked Ivy League favorite Pennsylvania in the first game of a Palestra doubleheader, 42-39.

The Gamecocks cooled off considerably after that, finishing with an 11-13 record, 4-10, in the conference, and defeated Clemson 60-52 in the opening round of the Atlantic Coast Conference tournament before bowing in the semi-finals to N. C. State, 75-72 on the Wolfpack's home floor.

The starting lineup of three sophomores, one junior and senior John Schroeder had four players average in double figures. Harlicka scored at a 14.3 pace, Salvadori at 13.8, Standard 13.0 and Thompson 10.8. Schroeder averaged 4.1 points per game. Standard was the rebounding leader with an average of 10.6.

Despite the near miss on a winning season, the groundwork had been laid for a resurgence in Gamecock basketball.

V

South Carolina

vs

Marquette

December 16, 1966---South Carolina 63, Marquette 61 (Milwaukee Classic)

at Milwaukee, Wisconsin

Despite what several journalists wrote in the mid 1960s, Al McGuire was not Frank McGuire's younger brother. They were not related, but they were close enough to be brothers.

Al and his brother, Dick, played for Frank McGuire at St. John's University. When Belmont Abbey, a small Catholic college at Belmont, N. C., near Charlotte, sought Frank McGuire's advice about employing a basketball coach, he recommended Al McGuire. When Marquette University sought Frank's recommendation, he also endorsed Al.

In Frank McGuire's third season of building a basketball program at the University of South Carolina, he would take his Gamecocks to the Milwaukee Classic, a four team December tournament, and Frank and Al would oppose each other for the first time.

South Carolina had come a long way from the 6-17 record of Frank McGuire's first year, but still had a long way to go. The Gamecocks had improved to an 11-13 record in the 1965-66 season, highlighted by a 73-71 upset win over then third ranked Duke. The media, in a pre-season poll, picked the Gamecocks to finish third in the Atlantic Coast Conference behind perennial favorites Duke and North Carolina.

South Carolina was strengthened by the return of 6-7, 235 pound Gary Gregor who had been ineligible for the previous one and a half seasons. He gave the Gamecocks a strong starting lineup that included 6-9 senior Al Salvadori and three juniors, 6-4 Frank Standard, 6-1 Skip Harlicka and 6-0 Jack Thompson.

Tom Farrell, a 6-4 New Yorker, had also joined the Gamecocks after being named a junior college All-America at Kilgore College in Texas.

The picture was clouded, however, by an eligibility controversy surrounding sophomore Mike Grosso, a 6-9 potential super star from Raritan, N.J. Some other ACC schools challenged Grosso's eligibility and he was eventually ruled ineligible to play at South Carolina.

Before the ruling, however, Grosso, in a pre-season scrimmage, suffered a severe knee injury that required surgery and would have probably been lost for the season anyway. He subsequently transferred to the University of Louisville where he had a successful career, settled, and became successful in radio and television advertising sales.

South Carolina won two home games and a conference game at Maryland in early December to take a 3-0 record to Milwaukee. The Gamecocks eased by Erskine 87-57, won a two point decision, 65-63, at Maryland and downed Furman 76-57. The Paladins' new head coach was their former All-America and two time national scoring champion Frank Selvy.

In addition to the McGuire versus McGuire matchup, there was another reunion on the basketball court at the Milwaukee Arena. South Carolina's Frank Standard and 6-2 Marquette guard George Thompson had been teammates in leading Brooklyn's Erasmus Hall High School to an undefeated season and a New York City championship.

Marquette entered the December 16 contest with a 3-2 record, having defeated Aquinas, South Dakota and New York University with losses to Villanova and Toledo. With the home court advantage, Marquette was considered a slight favorite.

The game was as close as its final two point margin indicated and developed into a physical struggle, described by writer Jeff Denberg of Columbia's *The State*, as "a war from the foul line and a case of physical strength against strength."

Four technical fouls were called against South Carolina, two on Frank Standard and two on the bench. Newspapers reported both were against Frank McGuire, but one was called against trainer Jim Price, who had some choice words for the officiating.

After the fourth technical, Al McGuire—walking on his knees from his bench to near mid-court—pleaded with the officials to call a technical foul on Marquette, saying "Every time you hit them with a T, then you kill us."

The refs were not amused, but refused the request and the game continued.

It boiled down to a two point South Carolina lead and a

Marquette possession with seconds remaining. A field goal would send the game into overtime. A shot from the corner hit the rim and bounced above the basket. Marquette's George Carbins crammed it into the net as the horn sounded to end regulation play.

One of the officials waved his arms frantically, yelling "No basket! No basket!." Carbins had put his hand in the cylinder to hit the basketball. That's basket interference against the offense, nullifying the basket. If the defense does it, its called goal tending, making the basket count.

Final score—South Carolina 63, Marquette 61.

The lead paragraph of Jeff Denberg's game story read: "Icy nerved South Carolina, brilliant under pressure and against adversity, knocked off favored Marquette with a second half comeback here Friday night to advance to the finals of the Milwaukee Classic."

Denberg added, "It was a 63-61 decision, a war from the foul line and a case of physical strength versus strength as the Gamecocks ran their unbeaten string to 4-0, but only after a goal tending call against Marquette's George Carbins with one second remaining.

"South Carolina was six points down in the second half after forging a 27-27 tie at intermission. It took Coach Frank McGuire's team almost half the period to catch up..."

Denberg singled out "a couple of new USC heroes" as instrumental in the victory, saying "First Tom Farrell and then Skip Harlicka made up for the woes besetting Gary Gregor and Jack Thompson."

Gregor picked up three personal fouls in the first eleven minutes of the game and received his fourth three seconds after the second half began. There were forty seven personal fouls called in addition to the four technicals. Thompson pulled a groin muscle early in the second half and played in pain the remainder of the game.

After trailing 34-28, South Carolina tied it at 40-40 on Harlicka's free throw. Farrell made two free throws to lift the Gamecocks to a 48-46 advantage with 7:12 left to play. Farrell tipped in a Standard miss and drove the base line to up the score to 52-47. The Gamecocks hung on from there to the final two point margin.

Farrell ended with 12 points and 15 rebounds. Harlicka led the South Carolina scoring with 19 points.

Bob Cole, writing in *The Columbia Record*, said "Frank McGuire stood quietly off to the side and tried to forget the four technical fouls called on him and his South Carolina Gamecocks. Across the room, Tom Farrell smiled."

Farrell told Cole, "maybe it was just adjusting to this group of guys—or something like that—but tonight was the first time I've gone out and been relaxed for an entire ball game. I've been tense up to now. I just feel good about being a part of this team and playing for Coach McGuire."

Several weeks later Farrell would suffer a severe knee injury and play no more for the Gamecocks.

McGuire said, "we had to spread it out and just like we had to go to the zone (2-1-2) when we got in foul trouble. They were too tough to defense man to man."

Gary Gregor set a school record with thirty five rebounds in a game.—*USC Sports Information*

The Gamecocks came a cropper the following night as the Milwaukee Classic retained its tradition of one of its "home" teams winning the championship. South Carolina lost to Wisconsin 88-84 despite 26 points by Skip Harlicka and 19 by Gary Gregor, who also pulled down 18 rebounds.

Playmaker Jack Thompson, hobbled by the groin muscle he pulled the night before, scored two points and Tom Farrell fouled out with ten minutes to play. Only UCLA, among the outside challengers, had been able to win the Milwaukee Classic.

Harlicka and Gregor were named to the all-tournament team. Two nights later, in Charlotte, N. C., Gregor would set a Charlotte Coliseum record as well as a South Carolina school record, by totaling 35 rebounds in a 102-78 South Carolina victory over Elon in a game added to the schedule after Duke canceled its games with the Gamecocks.

That was one of three occasions in which I, as sports information director, had a hand in a record.

The first was at Charlottesville, Va., during the 1968 football season. South Carolina led Virginia 49-28 and Coach Paul Dietzel had taken out all of his starters. About a minute remained in the game when I informed Coach Dietzel that Fred Zeigler had tied a school record with eleven pass receptions. Zeigler returned to the game, caught a screen pass for a one yard loss. It gave him a dozen receptions but, as we learned later, reduced his yardage for the game to 199. South Carolina to this day doesn't have an individual 200 yard reception game in football.

Gregor had 32 rebounds when I advised Coach McGuire the

school record was 33 set by Lee Collins against The Citadel in 1956. McGuire sent Gregor back in with instructions to "get two more rebounds and come out." He got three before the next dead ball.

That not only set a school record but bettered the Charlotte Coliseum record of 27 rebounds by Billy Cunningham of North Carolina.

The third occasion was in a 118-83 win over Furman in 1971 in the Carolina Coliseum. McGuire had removed his starters when I let him know John Roche had scored 52 points and the record was 54 set by Grady Wallace against Georgia in December 1956. Roche reentered the game, scored two quick field goals, and upped the record to 56 points.

After the Milwaukee Classic, South Carolina finished the 1966-67 season with a 16-7 record, the first of fourteen winning seasons under Frank McGuire. The Gamecock record in the Atlantic Coast Conference was 8-4 and in the ACC tournament at Greensboro. South Carolina defeated Maryland 57-54 before losing in the semi-finals to Duke, 69-66.

That was the only game between South Carolina and Duke that season as Blue Devil athletics director Eddie Cameron had canceled the two regular season games with the Gamecocks as a result of the eligibility dispute over Mike Grosso.

VI

South Carolina

vs

Cincinnati

December 22, 1967--South Carolina 64, Cincinnati 61
(Kentucky Invitational Tournament)
at Lexington, Kentucky

Entering the fourth season of Frank McGuire's rebuilding effort, the University of South Carolina basketball program was beginning to command some respect in the Atlantic Coast Conference.

The 1966-67 Gamecocks had posted a 16-7 record, the first winning season in five years. The "Four Horsemen"— Jack Thompson, Skip Harlicka, Frank Standard and Gary Gregor—were seniors, seasoned in the war of ACC competition. Joining them was a skinny, 6-2 sophomore with a fighting heart larger than his 160 pound body. His name was Bobby Cremins.

Jeff Denberg, basketball beat writer for *The State*, Columbia's morning newspaper, predicted North Carolina was an easy selection for the conference championship but Denberg thought South Carolina would battle Duke for second place.

In his pre-season analysis, Denberg said North Carolina, with 6-4 Charlie Scott and 6-3 Larry Miller "will benefit from having near seven footer Rusty Clark between them and they will both be better off if slick Eddie Fogler makes it at guard with Dick Grubar."

The writer added, "South Carolina and Duke will have fun fighting it out for second place. The Gamecocks have four proven seniors in guards Jack Thompson and Skip Harlicka and forwards Gary Gregor, the ACCs leading rebounder, and Frank Standard, who finished third to Gregor behind Duke's Mike Lewis" the previous season when the Gamecocks surprised everyone with a third place finish.

Denberg felt depth would be South Carolina's biggest obstacle.

"Were basketball strictly a five man game," he wrote, "South Carolina would have a tremendous team. But basketball isn't just for five guys...A prerequisite for success is a bench and the Game-

Action in the old Carolina Field House. Gary Gregor (40) demonstrates his unusual free throw shooting style. Other Gamecocks in the photo are Skip Harlicka (31) and Jack Thompson (44).
—USC Sports Information

cocks don't have one. This deficiency alone could keep an exciting team away from a spectacular season. That, and a pair of gimpy legs."

Thompson, the passing wizard and playmaker, had been hampered throughout his career by pulled groin muscles, bad ankles, and a series of other injuries, and began his senior season with serious blisters on his feet plus the lingering effects of muscle pulls.

Denberg conceded the Gamecocks had more than five competitive players, linking 6-8 Skip Kickey, "trimmed down to 210 pounds" with the Four Horsemen and Cremins.

"Frank McGuire's team goes better than five. He has six players he can count on. After that, the Gamecocks are in trouble." Seniors Al Salvadori and John Schroeder were gone from the 1966-67 squad and Bob Felter had dropped out of school.

Denberg described Thompson as "a magical playmaker," Harlicka, "a superb shooter," Standard, "a shifty inside sneak," and Gregor as "a truly wonderful talent." He said Kickey had recovered from a shoulder separation which ruined his junior season and should benefit from the loss of weight.

"McGuire can back up his guards with soph Bob Cremins, but he can expect little help from the remainder of last year's freshman team," Denberg concluded.

He described the Four Horsemen as a finely tuned quartet, adding "they are confident young men, almost cocky. They have in common their ability to play basketball and play it well."

The 1967-68 season was scheduled to be the last in the 41 year old, 3,200 capacity, Carolina Field House. As the Four Horsemen prepared for their senior campaign, the steel framework of the 12,401 seat Carolina Coliseum was rising at the corner of Columbia's Assembly and Blossom streets.

A talented freshman team with such names as John Roche, Tom Owens, John Ribock and Billy Walsh would make their varsity debuts in the new building the following year.

The Gamecocks tuned up by battering Erskine 104-54 in the season opener and Denberg wrote that Gregor and Standard "clobbered Erskine inside and a slick little thief named Bob Cremins hounded the Flying Fleet all over the floor."

However, Thompson remained on the bench in street clothes and Gregor came down with the 'flu as South Carolina traveled north for two conference games at Maryland and Virginia. The Gamecocks lost two heart breakers as a three point play by Billy Jones with seconds to play gave Maryland a 66-65 win, and South Carolina, battling from 18 points down, fell just short in an 84-82 setback at Virginia.

The Gamecocks rallied to trounce Furman 108-55 to take a 2-2 record to the University of Kentucky Invitational Tournament at Lexington three days before Christmas.

Kentucky, which had dominated its own holiday tournament with nine championships under Coach Adolph Rupp, was paired against Dayton, which had advanced to the NCAA title game against UCLA the previous March in the opening night second game after 15th ranked Cincinnati took on South Carolina.

The Gamecocks, especially with playmaker Jack Thompson still on the injured list, were considered the fourth best team in the strong field. Denberg wrote, "It may very well be when the season is over that three fourths of the field winds up in the NCAA regional playoffs or at least the NIT."

Rupp was at his best presiding over a pre-tournament luncheon, as described by writer Randy Laney of *The Columbia Record*:

"The Baron of Basketball was like a feudal overlord as he briefly scanned rustic Lexington before turning to address a gathering of sports writers and visiting school representatives in town for the 15th annual Kentucky Invitational Tournament."

Laney described Rupp as "simultaneously monarch and court jester" as he poked fun at visiting coaches Frank McGuire, Don Donoher of Dayton and Tay Baker of Cincinnati.

"Some folks have ventured to say we tried to pick a patsy as our first round opponent," Rupp declared. "Well, my friends, there ain't no patsies in this tournament."

Rupp seized upon a typographical error in Kentucky's media guide that listed South Carolina's enrollment as 63,000, rather than 13,000 to aim a jab at McGuire.

"I believe you ought to be able to find five kids who can play ball in a crowd like that," the Baron declared.

Cincinnati came into the tournament with a 4-1 record, having lost only to nationally ranked Kansas.

The Gamecocks and Bearcats went after each other tooth and nail with South Carolina falling behind 28-19 before outscoring Cincinnati 13-2 to take a one point halftime lead at 31-30. In the second half, the Gamecocks choked Cincinnati's offense with a 1-3-1 zone defense and surged to a 13 point lead before surviving a fierce press to claim a 64-61 decision.

The headline over Jeff Denberg's game story in *The State*, shouted: "USC Shatters Cincy Press to Grab Shocking 64-61 Win."

"South Carolina spit in the eye of Cincinnati's pressure defense here Friday night as the Gamecocks scored a rousing 64-61 upset victory to jump into the finals of the Kentucky Invitational against the local heroes in the house that Adolph built," is the way Denberg described it.

Kentucky, in the second game, outlasted Dayton 88-85, to reach the title game against the Gamecocks.

"It was a brilliant effort as South Carolina came from nine points down to take a 13 point lead and then hold on against a tough, defensive minded team that had previously lost only to nationally ranked Kansas," Denberg added.

"And, it was a night that belonged to Skip Harlicka, Gary Gregor and Frank Standard, with a huge assist from sophomores Bob Cremins and Gene Spencer."

Spencer, a seldom used 6-8 forward from Charleston, had come off the bench when Skip Kickey fouled out, and contributed six points, including four for four from the foul line, despite quickly picking up five personal fouls himself.

Gregor, fully recovered from his bout with the 'flu, scored 20 points and pulled down 15 rebounds. Harlicka, hitting 9 of 15 field goal attempts—many from long range—tallied 19, while Frank Standard scored 13 points and had 7 rebounds. Without playmaker Jack Thompson, however, the Gamecocks recorded only four assists, two each by Standard and Harlicka.

Rick Roberson, half of Cincinnati's 6-9 twin towers, scored 24 points for the Bearcats, 16 of them from the foul line. However, he made only 4 of 13 field goal attempts and was limited to 6 rebounds against South Carolina's 1-3-1 defense. Jim Ard, the other 6-9 tower, scored 9 points and had 7 rebounds

Coming into the tournament, Roberson led Cincinnati with a 15 points per game and 13 rebounds average. Ard was averaging 12 points and 10 rebounds and the three other starters—Gordon Smith, Don Ogletree and John Howard—each averaged 10.8 as the Bearcat scoring was evenly distributed.

Denberg said the Gamecocks were "dog tired after battling Cincinnati down to the wire." he said the Gamecocks had chances to put the game away several times in the final minutes but couldn't make free throws, finishing 14 for 23 from the line.

"Finally, Standard made his 12th and 13th points on a one and one with seven seconds left to put it away."

Although cold from the foul line, South Carolina shot 55.6 per cent from the floor, making 25 of 45 field goal attempts, including 59.1 per cent in the second half on 13 of 22. Cincinnati shot 38.5 per cent on field goals and made 21 of 31 free throws.

Frank McGuire was jubilant after the game, declaring, "Our kids played a beautiful, smart game. They were great. The zone did it. we had a 6-7 man (Gregor) and a 6-5 man (Standard) against two guys listed at 6-9 (Roberson and Ard). They're bigger than 6-9. We needed the zone and they did a great job with it."

He was particularly pleased with Gregor, saying "Gary did a tremendous job. He fought those big men off the boards. It was one of his greatest nights. Standard did a good job too.

"But, I really have to say I was proud of Harlicka. He never faltered. He and Cremins broke the press. Gary helped them later but it was Harlicka and Cremins."

McGuire called the win "really one of the best since I came to South Carolina."

The win over Cincinnati set up the near impossible task of facing Kentucky on its home court for the tournament championship. McGuire called a team meeting the following afternoon at the hotel. Free spirit Frank Standard was missing when a head count was taken.

Knowing full well his mischievous forward wasn't in the room, the Irishman asked the team manager, "Is everyone here?"

"Standard is missing," the manager answered.

"So, go find him," McGuire retorted, and the room was silent for some minutes until a sheepish Standard slinked into the room and took a back seat.

"So, where were you, Frank?"

Without hesitation the quick witted senior from Brooklyn replied, "Coach, I was down in the lobby arguing with a Kentucky guy that you were a greater coach than Rupp."

Even the Irishman broke into laughter and the meeting began.

After Cincinnati defeated Dayton in the consolation game, the Gamecocks got into foul trouble early and appeared too tired from their titanic win the night before, and dropped a 76-66 decision to the seventh ranked Wildcats, who had lost only 27 home games since 1943, a span of 25 years.

Thirty personal fouls were whistled against the Gamecocks and Kentucky cashed in 30 of 41 free throw attempts. There were 23 fouls called on Kentucky.

Mike Casey led the Wildcats with 19 points. Standard scored 24 for South Carolina, Cremins has 17, Harlicka 11, and Gregor 9 points along with a dozen rebounds, and made the all-tournament team. Standard also had 12 rebounds. Standard, Gregor, Harlicka and Skip Kickey all fouled out.

McGuire said his team "played our hearts out but Kentucky was too strong for us physically.

Adolph Rupp called it "a very vicious game. One of the hardest fought I have ever seen."

South Carolina returned home to face the ACC wars and rallied from its 0-2 start at Maryland and Virginia to post a 9-5 conference record, 15-7 overall.

And there would be two stupendous wins over top ten teams to come.

VII

South Carolina

vs

Duke

February 24, 1968--South Carolina 56, Duke 50

at Durham, North Carolina

South Carolina defeated Duke 83-80 at Columbia on January 30 and lost a close decision, 84-80, to North Carolina February 17 in the North-South doubleheaders at Charlotte, but still had to meet the two titans of Tobacco Road on their home courts before the 1968 season ended.

After upsetting Cincinnati and losing to Kentucky in the Kentucky Invitational tournament in December, the Gamecocks rattled off an eight game win streak which included seven Atlantic Coast Conference victories, two each over Wake Forest and Clemson, plus Maryland, Virginia and Duke.

After losses to N. C. State and North Carolina in the North-South Doubleheaders at Charlotte, South Carolina barely beat non-conference opponent Furman, 66-64, to take an 11-5 record, 7-4 in the conference, to Durham to meet eighth ranked Duke. Duke had won 18 of 22 games and hadn't lost since bowing to the Gamecocks more than three weeks earlier.

Duke's home record over the past eight years was 77-4 and Frank McGuire called Duke Indoor Stadium, "one of the toughest places in America on a visiting team."

The Gamecock win over the Blue Devils at Columbia had been a high scoring affair with both teams in the eighties, but few people thought South Carolina would try to run with the Blue Devils in Durham.

"You don't want to run with a team and get blown completely out of the yard," is the way Frank McGuire put it. Duke's previous opponent, Wake Forest, had resorted to a stall but still lost by nine points, 50-41.

As expected, the Gamecocks opened in deliberate fashion, passing the basketball 51 times between their second and third field goal attempts, holding the ball for 7 minutes and 47 seconds. The second shot was a jumper by Gary Gregor that scored and the third a 15 footer by Skip Harlicka.

Despite slowing the pace, South Carolina trailed by four at halftime, 19-15.

The Gamecocks fell nine points behind in the second half and trailed by seven, 39-32, when the pace quickened. The Gamecocks played flawless basketball while Duke went into a drought, going more than nine minutes without a field goal against South Carolina's man to man defense.

Frank Standard, Jack Thompson and Gary Gregor each scored to narrow the Duke lead to two points. Fearful of his passing skills, the Blue Devils played off Thompson in an attempt to block the passing lanes, despite the fact Thompson had scored 21 points in South Carolina's win at Columbia.

The loose defense left the Gamecock playmaker open and he again turned scorer, winding up with 22 on 10 field goals in 12 attempts and a couple of free throws.

Skip Harlicka's field goal gave South Carolina its first lead, 40-39. Thompson banked in a shot, and was alone on the base line for a layup and suddenly the Gamecock lead was five, 44-39. A free Throw by Bobby Cremins, a layup by Standard and another by Thompson all but closed the door. Thompson and Cremins made one and ones, Duke's Dave Golden scored, and South Carolina led by eight, 56-48, when Tim Teer of Duke scored with two seconds left on the clock.

Duke, which had never lost to South Carolina twice in the same season, stayed in the game only from the foul line, sinking 8 of 11 with Mike Lewis making 7 of his 19 points from the foul line. He was the only Duke player in double figures and also had 10 rebounds.

South Carolina, whose five starters played 40 minutes each while Duke used nine players, got 13 points from Harlicka, 10 from Cremins, who made 6 of 7 from the foul line, 6 from Gregor and 5 from Standard to support Thompson's 22.

Standard had nine rebounds but there weren't many off the Gamecock offensive board as South Carolina shot 62.9 per cent while Duke's field goal percentage was 42.9.

The headline in *The State* reported the upset this way: "Gamecock Battle Plan Shocks Blue Devils With Brilliant Second Half Comeback, 56-50."

Beat writer Jeff Denberg wrote, "Frank McGuire, a man with ice water in his veins, set up a game plan here Saturday night and South Carolina, a team with steel nerves, carried it out magnificently for a shocking 56-50 upset of Duke that has to rank among USCs greatest basketball wins."

Denberg added the Gamecocks "frustrated Duke with a long stall in the first half and then fell nine points down in the second before it happened, before they shot the eighth ranked Dukes dead."

Duke was "seemingly in no danger of losing at home for the fifth time in eight years," Denberg added, when South Carolina "began to play almost flawless basketball."

Bobby Cremins, a 53.4 per cent free throw shooter on the season, wasn't intimidated by the surroundings.

"The skinny sophomore, as poor a foul shooter as Wilt Chamberlain, stood out there throughout the final hectic minutes and knocked in one after another."

Denberg called it "an electric night from the moment it began, the kind of tense evening that makes palms sweat and kids scream from the stands in frustration."

Skip Harlicka recalled that Thompson, a married player and a new father, was at the foul line with the game still in doubt and Harlicka walked over and said "Hit these free throws for your son, Christian."

"That's Christian Michael," Thompson replied and then swished both attempts.

McGuire said in his post game statement, "There's nothing bigger than a victory over Duke at Duke. They've beaten some wonderful teams here."

The coach said his players "held their poise all the way and they played a fine man for man defense."

Duke coach Vic Bubas said the loss hurt, but "Its not the end of the world."

One personal note on this big Gamecock victory: It was cold in February and I had placed my overcoat on press row, which at Duke's old arena was located along the first row of the stands. When the game ended, I rushed to the locker room and when I returned, the top coat was gone. Some Duke fan was probably wearing my overcoat the next day, and I came back to Columbia a chilled but excited winner.

VIII

South Carolina

vs

North Carolina

February 28, 1968--South Carolina 87, North Carolina 86

at Chapel Hill, North Carolina

Strange things are supposed to happen during leap year, but two wins in four days over top ten opponents on the road seemed to be too much to ask, especially with both road trips taking South Carolina's Gamecocks to North Carolina's Tobacco Road.

Coach Frank McGuire and his Gamecocks had little time to savor the 56-50 upset of Duke on February 24 before heading back north for a February 28 date with Coach Dean Smith's North Carolina Tar Heels.

The Duke assignment was tough, but this one was tougher. North Carolina's record was 21-1, 12-0 in the conference, and a 20 game win streak. The Tar Heels had won 17 consecutive decisions over Atlantic Coast Conference opponents—including three in the 1967 ACC tournament—since losing to South Carolina 70-57 at Columbia March 1 the previous year.

South Carolina's record stood at 13-5, 8-4 in the ACC.

North Carolina had never lost in Carmichael Auditorium, its new facility winding up its second season. The Tar Heels had beaten the Gamecocks in Charlotte eleven days earlier, although by only four points, 84-80. No one expected the Gamecocks to score 80 points in Chapel Hill. In fact, most thought the Gamecocks would stall; hold the ball like they did in the first half at Duke.

Bob Cole, writing in *The Columbia Record*, said "Frank McGuire's not saying but it wouldn't be a bad guess that the University of South Carolina basketball coach has something up his sleeve for tonight's invasion of Tar Heel Country.

"South Carolina has been basking in the warmth of a surprising 56-50 upset victory over Duke that saw South Carolina slow things down and play a controlled, non-aggressive attack."

Cole added, "For this one, McGuire has several options...none of which offer much of a guarantee against a team that has not lost since December 9."

The writer said the Gamecock slowdown against Duke "worked simply because the Blue Devils allowed them to take their time in the early going and never really tried to pressure them, until it was too late. North Carolina, particularly playing on its home floor, is not likely to stand for such foolishness."

"We can't run against them," Frank McGuire said, lending credence to the theory the Gamecocks would hold the ball. "They're going to press us all over the court and it will be a case of us trying to get through their press."

Jeff Denberg, in his pre-game story in *The State*, wrote, "South Carolina is faced with an almost impossible task tonight. The Gamecocks go into what is known as Blue Heaven to play North Carolina, the third ranked college basketball team in America, a team that has bowled over 20 straight opponents.

"It will be a miracle if the Gamecocks win and maybe two miracles in the space of five days is too much to expect, but Frank McGuire has a handful of characters who don't think so."

Denberg said the Gamecocks were sensational against Duke and "they will have to be just as wonderful tonight and they certainly aren't awed by the task at hand."

South Carolina playmaker Jack Thompson, who had ten assists in the four point loss to the Tar Heels at Charlotte, was coming off perhaps his finest game in the win at Duke, but was still bothered by blistered feet.

Eleven years earlier, in a different building—Woolen Gymnasium—Frank McGuire had coached North Carolina to a national championship. He received a standing ovation from the Tar Heel crowd when introduced as the Gamecock head coach.

North Carolina also introduced Dennis Wuycik, a blue chip prospect from Pennsylvania on his recruiting visit, and honored the seniors playing their final home game.

Every seat in Carmichael Auditorium was filled and several hundred were seated on the floor behind the baskets and the cheerleaders. I remember spotting South Carolina swimming coach Jack Thompson—no relation to the basketball player—and members of his team in the throng and wondered how they got in. The swim team was in Chapel Hill for a meet with the Tar Heels.

It turned out Thompson, who had a six foot eight inch swimmer who looked like a basketball player, had lined his tall free styler up ahead of shorter swimmers and blurted "freshman team" as he hustled them past the attendant guarding the players' entrance.

The Gamecocks didn't stall. They challenged the Tar Heels and found themselves seven points behind at the half, 43-36. Down 13 points early in the second half, the Gamecocks outscored the Tar Heels 19-4, led 79-70 with 2:46 remaining, and then held on for dear life for the win.

As Jeff Denberg wrote, "The sacrificial lamb got up from the altar and slit the executioner's throat. Little Bobby Cremins, admittedly "the worst free shooter on the team," did it again. After making 6 of 7 from the foul line in the win over Duke, Cremins dropped 13 of 16 at Chapel Hill, including 5 in a row in the final minute and a half, to save an 87-86 South Carolina victory.

Denberg said in past years South Carolina had been a program "always invited for homecomings and awards presentations and one always thought someone was missing the boat by not scheduling them for weddings and bar mitzvahs."

He said "Little Cremins was beautiful, making foul shots and bringing the ball up. Gregor was magnificent in the second half, surprising himself—but no one else—with his work inside. Thompson was running full steam, dealing out passes like Standard deals out cards."

Frank Standard was the card shark on the team, along with various other off the court skills.

When the smoke cleared, South Carolina had outscored North Carolina 51-43 in the second half, had made 33 of 62 field goal attempts in the game for 53.2 per cent, and was 21 of 27 from the foul line, 77.8 per cent. The Gamecocks even outrebounded the Tar Heels, 43-38. North Carolina made only 39.8 per cent of its field goal attempts and shot 71.4 per cent from the foul line.

North Carolina three times in the final minute cut South Carolina's lead to two points and then fouled Cremins to send the 53.4 per cent shooter to the foul line. Twice he calmly sank both free throws to boost the margin back to four. With five seconds remaining, he sank his fifth straight for a three point lead, then missed and the Gamecocks cleared out to avoid a foul, and gave North Carolina an unchallenged two points for the final, 87-86, margin.

Cremins, on 13 of 16 free throws and 5 of 10 field goals, had 23 points, matched by Skip Harlica's 9 of 16 field goals and 5 of 7 free throws. Frank Standard scored 18 points, Gary Gregor 15 and Jack Thompson 8, in addition to turning in 7 assists. However, Harlicka out assisted his back court mate with 9.

Cremins, all six feet two, 160 pounds of him, grabbed an amazing 15 rebounds, while Gregor corralled 12 and Standard grabbed 7. Five Gamecock reserves got into the game, but all the points and all but three of the rebounds were by the starters.

North Carolina's five starters scored all of the Tar Heel points also. Larry Miller had 26, Rusty Clark 18, Charlie Scott 16, Dick Grubar 15, and Bill Bunting 11. The seven foot Clark pulled down 15 rebounds.

One of the four Tar Heels subs in the game was sophomore guard Eddie Fogler, who played seven minutes and had one assist. Twenty five years later he would be South Carolina's head coach while Dean Smith would still be going strong at North Carolina. Bobby Cremins would be racking up wins as an ACC opponent of Smith at Georgia Tech.

In the Gamecock locker room Jack Thompson—the basketball player, not the swim coach—shook his head as he looked at Cremins.

"I don't believe you, Bobby. I just don't believe the things you do."

Jubilation reigned in the victorious South Carolina locker room. Assistant coach Donnie Walsh, a former North Carolina player under both Frank McGuire and Dean Smith and a graduate of the UNC Law School, was thrown into the shower fully clothed. The players didn't get up enough nerve to douse the head coach, but the Irishman let his guard down enough to loosen his tie and remove his jacket.

In the North Carolina locker room Coach Dean Smith said "The defeat was tough for us but I hope we go as long again between defeats. That young man Cremins is a fine player."

McGuire said "North Carolina might have been a little tight. That long winning streak had to be a burden on them but they are a great team."

Jeff Denberg, in a follow up story, said "Yes, miracles do happen in Blue Heaven. South Carolina was reeling into oblivion...Then, all of a sudden rose up and swatted down third ranked North Carolina's twenty game winning streak."

The maker of the miracle, Denberg added, "was little Bobby Cremins, a skinny sophomore who is all guts. Stuck on the foul line under unbelievable pressure while his house was collapsing around him, he made free throw after free throw — five in all — to dump North Carolina's fantastic last minute press and save the evening.

Herman Helms, executive sports editor of *The State*, made the trip on the team charter plane and his March 1 column, two days after the historic victory, said "The Four Horsemen and the Kid did it."

The Four Horsemen, of course, were Gregor, Standard, Thompson and Harlica. The Kid was Bobby Cremins.

"The Four Horsemen and the Kid and a senior sub who came off the bench and met a time of emergency with savvy," Helms related. The senior sub was 6-8 Skip Kickey, pressed into service when both

Standard and Gregor fouled out in the final five minutes. Kickey didn't score but he contributed two key rebounds and an assist.

"They knocked off mighty North Carolina, third ranked basketball team in the nation and the winner of 20 straight games, in a game at Chapel Hill Wednesday night that was almost too thrilling to believe.

"Four nights earlier, they had upended eighth ranked Duke, 56-50, in Durham. In five days these incredible South Carolina Gamecocks stuck the dagger in the third and eighth ranked teams in the nation, and to make it even more of a fairy tale, they did it on the opposition's home floor."

The two victories brought an estimated 5,000 delirious Gamecock fans to the Columbia airport to meet the team after midnight on its return from Chapel Hill.

The two wins, Helms wrote, "revealed a master coach at his very best."

"It is something you hope for and pray for and dream about," McGuire said on the flight home. "But, it doesn't happen, beating Duke and North Carolina back to back on their home floors when they've got great teams. It just doesn't happen, but it did.

"If anybody had come to me and told me it would happen, I would have said, 'listen, fellow, you're crazy.' It was a thousand to one shot."

South Carolina athletics director Paul Dietzel, who was also head football coach, made the trip and was interviewed by Helms on the flight home.

"I don't want to stick myself in this. This was a basketball victory, a tremendous victory and no football coach has any business sharing the stage," Dietzel said.

"But, I can't keep it to myself, I've got to say it. This is the most remarkable job of coaching I've ever seen. The way those kids held their poise and kept coming back was something to see. That has to be coaching; super coaching!"

Helms said it would be unfair "and totally inaccurate" to pick out one player who won the game, because "victories of this magnitude obviously come from the efforts of many."

He said the Four Horsemen played "the way seniors should, had kept their cool under pressure that was unbearably heavy."

However, "Fate put the burden of this game on the shoulders of the kid at the finish and the kid—the calm and beautiful kid—saved it."

On the final trip to the foul line, Helms said Cremins calmly lined up while the North Carolina crowd, which "had been splendid up until then" hooted and jeered.

Bobby Cremins (center), a South Carolina sophomore in the old Carolina Field House in 1968, and (right) as Georgia Tech's head coach more than 25 years later.*—USC Sports Information; Georgia Tech Sports Information*

"When the kid—little Bobby Cremins, sophomore Bobby Cremins—had the game in his hands to win or lose, their emotions got the best of the UNC fans. They stomped and they whistled and jeered as he stood there facing the basket. Facing the most challenging moment of his young life.

"He pumped and he let it go, the first shot of a one and one. The ball dropped cleanly in the basket and that was it."

In a story written for *The Charlotte News*, Bill Ballenger observed:

"They named the All-ACC team today and among the many names not mentioned on its rolls was that of South Carolina's Bob Cremins.

"This is doubtless because Cremins is only 6-2, can't shoot, scores little and generally gets lost in the box scores with the substitutes.

"But, if there were to be an all-tough team named for the conference, Bobby Cremins would lead all the rest."

As an explanation, Ballenger quoted Coach Frank McGuire, "This kid plays basketball. He works at it 100 per cent, he never stops and all he'll say to you is, 'Coach, I'll do better'."

Teams lose to South Carolina and don't understand what's beating them, Ballenger stated.

"Cremins. He could lose himself in a broom closet."

Three days after beating North Carolina, South Carolina played its final game in the 41 year old Carolina Field House and the final home game for the Four Horsemen. The Gamecocks lost a heartbreaker to North Carolina State, 55-54.

In the ACC tournament at Charlotte, the Gamecocks routed Virginia 101-78 before meeting North Carolina for a third time that season in the semi-finals. Another thriller ensued with the Tar Heels eking out a three point decision, 82-79.

North Carolina, which lost at Duke by the same score as its defeat at the hands of South Carolina, 87-86, at Durham in the last regular season game, swept through the ACC tournament and NCAA regional, and defeated Ohio State in the final four before losing the national championship to perennial champion UCLA to finish with a 28-4 record.

South Carolina finished 15-7 and looked forward to moving into the new Carolina Coliseum the following season.

The Four Horsemen left a legacy of excellence. All of them scored in double figures for the year, Harlicka leading the way with a 21.8 average. Gregor averaged 15.6, Standard 13.8 and Thompson 10.9. Despite missing six games with injuries, Thompson had 72 assists in an era when the definition of an assist was much more difficult. For his career, Thompson had 294 career assists.

Gregor's .535 field goal percentage was a school record and South Carolina's .488 team percentage led the conference. Ten of South Carolina's games were decided by four points or less.

After the 82-79 loss to North Carolina in the ACC tournament semi-finals that ended their collegiate careers, Herman Helms wrote the quartet "went out blasting—with style."

McGuire said "I hate to see the kids pack it up. They have been soldiers, real soldiers. I've never seen a ball club with so much guts. They deserve to be national champions. They would be national champions if we had a big man to go with them."

IX

South Carolina

vs

Auburn

November 30, 1969--South Carolina 51, Auburn 49

at Columbia

The Four Horsemen were gone and "The Kid" was the captain, surrounded by a cast of four talented sophomores as South Carolina entered a new chapter in its basketball history.

The 41 year old Carolina Field House was also gone, destroyed by fire three weeks after the final home game of the 1967-68 season. Construction of the new Carolina Coliseum was accelerated and workmen were still bolting down seats half an hour before the scheduled tipoff of the 1968-69 season against Auburn of the Southeastern Conference.

Not all of the parking areas were paved and some of the other amenities were unfinished, but the Tartan floor was down and the goals were up and the cry was "Let the game begin."

While South Carolina was moving into its new coliseum, a new Madison Square Garden was opening in New York City. Frank McGuire recalled in an interview with Mel Derrick of *The Charlotte Observer* that he played in the first college game promoted by Ned Irish in the previous garden while a student at St. John's University.

"It was 1934," he remembered. "I was the second man on the court They had some curtains there for us to run through and nobody knew what was on the other side. We were used to playing before 2,000 people, maybe 3,000. I came through the curtains and there were 18,000 yelling at me. My first impulse was to turn and run back."

The Four Horsemen—seniors from South Carolina's 1968-69 team—had moved on to professional basketball or other pursuits.

Gary Gregor was the first round draft choice of the Phoenix Suns and made the National Basketball Association's all-rookie team. Skip Harlicka was the first round draft of the Atlanta Hawks and played one season in the NBA before returning to live in the Carolinas.

Jack Thompson played briefly with the ABA Indiana Pacers before injuries forced him out of basketball and he became a stock broker in New Orleans. He eventually moved back to Columbia.

Frank Standard went to Europe with the Spanish national team before becoming a "Sky Marshal" in the federal battle against aircraft hijackers. When that program was phased out, Standard became a U. S. Customs agent.

The Kid, junior Bobby Cremins, was named captain of a Gamecock squad that listed six sophomores, six juniors and no seniors. A starting lineup that had been billed as the Four Horsemen and The Kid, became the Four Sophs and a Junior.

Columnist Russell Borjes of the Norfolk *Virginian-Pilot* remembered Bobby Cremins from Bobby's days at Frederick Military Academy in nearby Portsmouth, Va., and he telephoned Cremins at his dormitory room.

"I never thought I would go to college much less play basketball. I grew up in a neighborhood where no one ever thought of going to college. I was the only white kid in the neighborhood," Cremins told Borjes.

"When I was 13 there was pot going all around and I used to watch grown men shooting with guns and using chains. It was on 149th street and it was like another Harlem."

After starring for All Hallows High School in New York City, Cremins spent a year in prep school at Frederick Military where he was accidentally "discovered" by South Carolina Coach Frank McGuire.

Frederick played Bullis Prep in a preliminary game to a South Carolina-Maryland contest at College Park. Cremins recalled that McGuire came to watch another player but "I scored 27 points and he talked to me afterwards."

That's how Bobby Cremins wound up at the University of South Carolina and became the Gamecock team captain as a junior. He would serve again as captain his senior year, earn a master's degree, and become a successful head basketball coach at Appalachian State University and Georgia Tech.

"The more I see that kid play," McGuire said of his 6-2, 160 pound captain, the better I like what he does. We wouldn't have won half the games we've won without him. He simply has no fear of bigger men."

The four sophomores joining Cremins in the starting lineup included high school teammates Tom Owens and John Roche from Manhattan's LaSalle Academy, Billy Walsh of Mamaroneck, N. Y., and John Ribock, a 6-8, 240 pound "enforcer" from Augusta, Ga.

Sports editor Jim Anderson of *The Greenville News* described

Coach Frank McGuire and his four sophomores and a junior starting five of 1968-69. *Kneeling (L-R):* Billy Walsh, Coach McGuire, John Roche. *Standing:* Junior Captain Bobby Cremins, Tom Owens, John Ribock.
—Tom Price Files

Owens as "two inches shy of being a seven footer" and "about 23 pounds shy of weighing what he should."

South Carolina assistant coach Buck Freeman said Owens would "rather be 6-8 but he's 6-10. He's underweight at 187."

The 6-10 Owens and 6-3 Roche perfected their "pick and roll" style at LaSalle Academy and brought it south when they signed with South Carolina.

"They have a very clever maneuver," Freeman said, "in which Tom sets the screen and winds up with John's man. It's then a 6-10 man against one only 6-1, usually."

That maneuver would help South Carolina win 69 basketball games over the next three seasons.

Freeman said "Roche may be the leader. Not only does he score well, but he is very good on defense. So is Walsh. They don't get trapped too much on the screen."

The sellout crowd for the first game in Carolina Coliseum was announced at 12,088. Capacity was soon raised to 12,401 when Dr. Thomas F. Jones, university president, had additional seats crammed beneath the rafters in the four corners of the arena. They were the worst seats in the house and dubbed "Dr. Jones specials" by students.

"The building was excellent, the crowd was big and noisy and had a gasser of a finish," was the way executive sports editor Herman Helms of *The State* described the first game in "The House That Frank Built."

"Sophomore John Roche made Saturday night a perfect opening night at the new Carolina Coliseum by pouring in a jump shot with two seconds left to vault South Carolina's Gamecocks past Auburn, 51-49," Helms said in his sidebar story.

"A beaming and perspiring Frank McGuire stood in the USC dressing room moments after the thriller had ended and uttered a considerable understatement."

Helms quoted McGuire as saying, "What a way to open a new building. But I didn't plan it this way. I'm not that good a script writer."

Captain Bobby Cremins sought out Roche, declaring "I'm thinking about kissing that boy. John will never know what that shot meant to all of us. I think it could be the thing that will make our season."

McGuire said he wanted Roche or the other guard, Billy Walsh, to take the last shot, but we told them to take it right at the game's end."

After a free throw by Cremins and a tap in by Owens had pulled South Carolina even from a three point deficit with 49 seconds on the clock, the Gamecocks regained possession and called a time out.

South Carolina had led most of the game only to fall behind with three and a half minutes remaining.

"We had this game won. Then we lost it. Then we won it back again," McGuire said. He added Auburn was a physical team and "They worked us over pretty good in the final half. They are so strong they just shut us off from the basket in the second half.

"One thing is very apparent about our team. We are going to have trouble with stamina. Our boys were getting very tired at the finish."

John Roche, shown here scoring against Auburn, was a three-time All-America guard.—*USC Sports Information*

Helms noted, "It is no secret that the Gamecocks, who started four sophomores with Cremins, are thin on the bench. They were particularly thin Saturday night due to a siege of mononucleosis which hit several of the players."

Beat writer Jeff Denberg of *The State* described the winning basket: "With the game tied and the Gamecocks playing for the final shot, Roche took the ball, drove to his right and got the shot off. The ball hit the rim, bounced against the backboard and finally fell through to set off a scene of pandemonium in the coliseum."

South Carolina held a ten point lead, 36-26, at halftime and maintained that margin into the second half when the Gamecocks suddenly went cold. A twisting layup by Auburn's Wallace Tinker tied the score at 46-46 with 4:39 remaining.

Tinker's tap in gave the War Eagles a two point lead that stretched to three, 49-46, on Ronnie Jackson's free throw with the clock showing 2:36, but that was all the scoring for Auburn.

Roche missed a free throw with 1:12 remaining but Cremins grabbed the rebound and was fouled. He made the first of a one and one, missed the second, and Owens tapped in the rebound to tie the score, 49-49.

When Auburn turned the ball over with 49 seconds to play, McGuire called a time out to set up the final shot.

Owens led South Carolina's scoring with 16 points and rebounding with 14. Roche scored 14, Cremins 11, Walsh 5 and John Ribock 4. The only point off the South Carolina bench was a free throw by guard Hank Martin. Jackson scored 19 for Auburn and sophomore John Mengelt had 12.

The State sent general assignment writer Jay A. Gross to cover the opening of the new coliseum, which he described as the largest arena in the Southeast "pressed into service before contractors could put on the finishing touches."

Gross quoted one woman fan as warning her son, "Don't touch that, it's probably wet cement."

From floor to ceiling, said Gross, "there is vast space," and he went on to say "the immensity of the coliseum doesn't fail to impress the spectators."

Gross quoted one fan as saying, "I never thought it would make it on time. It's sure an improvement over the Field House."

X

South Carolina

vs

LaSalle

December 30, 1968---South Carolina 62, LaSalle 59
(Quaker City Classic Championship)

at Philadelphia, Pa.

After opening the 1968-69 season and the Carolina Coliseum with a two point win over Auburn, South Carolina defeated Wake Forest on the road, Maryland and East Carolina at home, but lost road games to Virginia and Davidson to take a 4-2 record to the Quaker City Classic in Philadelphia.

The tournament had been a fixture and a sellout for many years at the 7,500 seat Palestra on the University of Pennsylvania campus but in 1967, the classic was moved to the much larger and more modern Spectrum, home court of the NBA Seventy Sixers. Attendance dropped sharply despite the larger and newer facility.

South Carolina defeated Rhode Island, 86-68, in the opening round of the eight team tournament, and then upset St. Joseph's—one of the local entries—64-58, to reach the championship game against unbeaten LaSalle, coached by former NBA star Tom Gola, who played for Frank McGuire when the Irishman coached the Philadelphia Warriors.

Attendance in the Spectrum, across town from the previous site at the Palestra, was disappointing, prompting Ray Kelly to write in the Philadelphia *Evening Bulletin*:

"Unless some people turn out for the tripleheader...there's going to be some unfavorable comment. Saturday night, only 5,018 showed up as South Carolina upset St. Joseph's and LaSalle crushed Indiana. And the weather wasn't that bad."

Kelly said one South Carolina rooter took a long look around the plush arena and said in a Dixie drawl, "We get bigger crowds than this for our practice games."

Kelly pointed out the 1968 Quaker City Classic had an attractive championship game "in which LaSalle's gung-ho shooters bid for national recognition against what is undoubtedly the most talented young team in the country. Moreover, Gola will be matching strategy with his former (and favorite) coach from the Philadelphia Warriors, dapper Frank McGuire."

The Gamecocks, said Kelly, "have a prime candidate for the tournament's most valuable player award in 19 year old John Roche. This 6-2 back courter is a do it all type and handles the main offensive chores for the Gamecocks along with another 19 year old, Tom Owens, a 6-10 center."

Assistant sports editor Bob Cole covered the tournament for *The State*, and his lead on the championship game said:

"South Carolina's Gamecocks, playing a controlled, patterned offense, fought off a menacing LaSalle press in the waning moments to trip the 11th ranked Explorers, 62-59, and capture the Quaker City Classic basketball tournament..."

Cole added the Gamecocks, who led by 12 points in the second half, "called on guard John Roche to lead the deliberate offense, and Roche responded by pumping in 24 points. Roche's performance netted him Most Valuable Player honors by an overwhelming margin."

South Carolina led by a dozen on three occasions, with 17:01 remaining and two minutes later when the score was 45-33. After LaSalle cut it to seven on baskets by Ken Durrett, Roche hit a free throw, banked in a jump shot and hit another jumper to boost the lead to 50-38 with 12:34 remaining.

Gola's team went into a full court press against the tiring Gamecocks and pared the lead to four points, 56-52, on baskets by Durrett and Larry Cannon with less than five minutes to play.

Bobby Cremins, Tom Owens and Billy Walsh all missed the front end of one and ones, giving the Explorers opportunities to further close the gap, but LaSalle gained only one point, on a free throw by Cannon. When he missed his second attempt, Owens cleared the rebound and South Carolina's lead was 56-53 with 2:12 to go.

John Ribock got loose for a layup but missed and LaSalle was still alive. Moments later, Roche again found Ribock loose under the basket and this time he scored to increase the lead to five points, 58-53.

Bernie Williams hit from the key at 1:03 to cut it back to three. Walsh cashed in two free throws with 54 seconds left, 60-55, Gamecocks. Williams quickly closed it to three again with a long bomb from the side.

Ribock, who had 11 rebounds in the game, made two free throws with 25 seconds to play, followed by Cannon's layup for LaSalle. The clock ran out with the scoreboard reading South Carolina 62, LaSalle 59.

South Carolina made 19 field goals on 35 attempts for 54.3 per cent shooting. The Gamecocks played a tight zone defense until the waning seconds, frustrating the efforts by LaSalle to run. As a result, the Explorers shot only 39.1 per cent, 27 of 69.

The zone defense kept South Carolina's fouls to a minimum and LaSalle went to the line only seven times, making five. South Carolina converted 24 of 30 free throw attempts.

Bob Lipper, in *The Charlotte Observer*, called the Gamecock style, Grand Central Station type basketball, pointing out South Carolina scored only one field goal the final twelve and a half minutes of the game, but still managed to win.

LaSalle, winner of eight straight before falling to the Gamecocks but barred from NCAA post season play due to probation, didn't lose another game and finished with a 24-1 record under Gola.

Tom Owens led the Atlantic Coast Conference in rebounding three consecutive years.
—USC Sports Information

Owens joined Roche on the all-tournament team along with Calvin Murphy of Niagara, Mike Hauer of St. Joseph's, Joe Cooke of Indiana and Cannon of LaSalle.

South Carolina's five starters again played iron man roles, each logging 40 minutes. Following Roche's 24 points, which included 10 of 11 from the foul line, Owens and Walsh scored 12 points each. Ribock had 9 and Bobby Cremins 7. Cremins again belied his reputation as a poor free throw shooter by making 5 of 6, but his one miss in the waning moments caused some anxiety.

Roche had eight assists in addition to his game leading 24 points.

"Frank McGuire, a passle of victories, championships and exhilarating moments behind him throughout the years, never beamed brighter than he did Monday night in Philadelphia's Spectrum," Bob Cole wrote in a sidebar story.

"A veteran of college and professional coaching wars that include a national championship while at North Carolina, McGuire is the mother hen of the South Carolina basketball squad, a fuzzy-cheeked bunch of kids who make the most difficult tasks appear downright easy.

"That's because they have a wealth of talent and, perhaps just as important, they do as they are told."

McGuire backed up Cole's observation by saying, "these kids are disciplined. They do what you tell them to do. And we did the only thing we could have done against a team like LaSalle. If we had tried to run, LaSalle would have scored a hundred and we might have gotten 60 or 70 points."

The South Carolina offense centered around breaking John Roche loose with the aid of a double pick, and the strategy worked to perfection.

"Roche gave a professional performance," McGuire declared. "The idea was to create a one on one situation with Roche moving around the two picks. We feel that he can beat anyone one-on-one."

Roche, in a locker room interview, analyzed the three point victory over LaSalle and the Explorers' nearly successful full court press.

"We looked up and saw we had a 12 point lead in the second half and began trying to hang onto it," he said. "We shouldn't have done that."

His coach agreed, saying, "In the final nine minutes we didn't go to the basket enough. I didn't want them to stop trying to score. But, how long can five guys keep going against a press like LaSalle threw at us?"

Apparently, opined sportswriter Bob Cole, "Just long enough to win."

South Carolina went on to a 21-7 record for the 1968-69 season, the Gamecocks' first 20 win season. In the Atlantic Coast Conference Tournament at Charlotte, the Gamecocks defeated Maryland 92-71, but lost in the semi-finals to Duke 68-59.

John Roche averaged 23.6 points per game and was voted the Atlantic Coast Conference Player of the Year. Roche's name was among the top five on every one of the 87 ballots cast for the all-conference team. Tom Owens, who led the conference in rebounding, was named to the second team.

Frank McGuire was named ACC Coach of the Year.

South Carolina received its first bid to the National Invitation Tournament in New York City's Madison Square Garden. The Gamecocks defeated Southern Illinois 72-63, but lost in the second round to Coach Bobby Knight's Army team, 59-45.

A freak accident cost the Gamecocks the services of sophomore guard Billy Walsh for the Army game, and Coach Frank McGuire's bench thin squad was unable to compensate for the loss. While leaving the Hotel New Yorker for a noon shoot around at the Garden, Walsh's equipment bag jammed a revolving door. The door's glass shattered and a shard of glass cut into one of Walsh's legs, requiring more than 50 stitches. Billy Walsh left school after his sophomore season and never played for the Gamecocks again.

XI

South Carolina

vs

Notre Dame

Dec. 30, 1969---South Carolina 84, Notre Dame 83 (OT)
(Sugar Bowl Tournament Championship)

at New Orleans, La.

As South Carolina prepared for the 1969-70 season, Bobby Cremins was back as a senior serving his second term as team captain. Billy Walsh was gone but the three other super sophomores—John Roche, Tom Owens and John Ribock—were back for their junior seasons.

They were joined by a 6-10 sophomore named Tom Riker, who had been one of the nation's most heavily recruited high school seniors the previous year. The availability of Riker to play center permitted Frank McGuire to move the skinny, 6-10 Owens to his more natural forward position.

Riker was from Hicksville, N. Y., and played at Oyster Bay High School. During the height of the recruiting season, a *New York Times* story written by Sam Goldaper reported, Riker "favors North Carolina with South Carolina his second choice."

When signing time came around, however, Riker chose Coach Frank McGuire's Gamecocks and sports editor Bill Brill of *The Roanoke Times*, a close follower of the recruiting wars, called the 6-10 left handed hook shooter "the biggest catch of all."

After a banner season with the freshman team, Riker's move to the varsity—along with the return of four starters from 1968-69—resulted in the Associated Press ranking the Gamecocks number one in its pre-season poll. Another key addition was 6-7 sophomore forward Rick Aydlett of Blacksburg, Va.

The number one ranking lasted just two games, however. South Carolina opened on the road with an easy win over Auburn, 84-63, but in the home opener at Carolina Coliseum, the Gamecocks suf-

Frank McGuire discusses strategy during practice with Bobby Cremins, Bob Carver, John Roche and Tom Owens.—***USC Sports Information***

fered a one point loss, 55-54, at the hands of Tennessee. South Carolina tumbled to eighth in the rankings.

That was followed by five straight wins, including an 89-52 Madison Square Garden victory over Long Island University in which South Carolina's homecoming New Yorkers, John Roche, Tom Owens and Tom Riker, scored 27, 20 and 20 points, respectively, and the forgotten New Yorker, captain Bobby Cremins, totaled 9.

McGuire then took his team to New Orleans for the Sugar Bowl Tournament, Dec. 29-30. South Carolina's football team was in Atlanta at the same time to play West Virginia in the Peach Bowl.

South Carolina led New Mexico 50-20 in the first half and routed the Lobos 85-62 to set up a showdown with Notre Dame for the Sugar Bowl championship. Roche, despite having bruised ribs which team physician, Dr. Emmett Lunceford, said would "be sore for a month," scored 31 points, making 14 of 19 field goal attempts plus 3 of 5 free throws. Owens and Rick Aydlett supplemented Roche by scoring 16 points each.

Roche credited his season high point total to the improved play of Riker and Aydlett.

"As each game goes by Riker and Aydlett learn where I am more," he said. "When you are playing with new people it just takes a little longer to get used to each other. I think the reason we have looked so good the last three games is because we are getting more used to each other. I probably have a higher percentage in the last few games because the defense is having to pick up Riker and Aydlett more."

The Irish, led by super star Austin Carr, downed West Virginia 84-80 to reach the title game.

It could have been called the "Pope Classic," or the "Rosary Bowl," Frank McGuire's team of predominantly Catholics from New York against the Fighting Irish from South Bend, Ind., except for one thing: Austin Carr was a Baptist.

With a 6-1 record going into the New Orleans tournament, the Gamecocks had moved up in the polls, to fifth a week before, and then third in both the Associated Press and United Press International polls. Notre Dame, also 6-1 entering the tournament, was ranked 11th by the AP and 13th by UPI.

The fourth race at New Orleans' fairgrounds track on Dec. 30, 1969, was named "South Carolina Gamecocks," and was won by a three year old filly named Burning Broom. The silks worn by jockey Leroy Moyers were Garnet and White. A $2 ticket on Burning Broom to win paid $8.

After West Virginia disposed of New Mexico 95-91 in the consolation game, the Gamecock basketball team found the going a little tougher than jockey Moyers and Burning Broom and trailed Notre Dame by 2 points, 75-73, with 14 seconds remaining in regulation before a capacity crowd of 4,720 in the old Loyola University Field House.

Not to worry. John Roche was at the foul line. He made two free throws and the game went into overtime. Roche sank four more free throws in the overtime period and when it was over, South Carolina had edged Notre Dame 84-83 to claim the Sugar Bowl Tournament championship.

While Roche made the clutch free throws that cemented the victory, his 25 points were the third most in the game and second among the Gamecocks. Carr scored 43 points on 19 field goals and 5 of 5 free throws for Notre Dame and was named the tournament's Most Valuable Player.

Sophomore Tom Riker, in the first of many big games in his South Carolina career, had 15 field goals and 6 of 7 from the foul line to tally 36 points. Riker had made only six points the night before in the win over New Mexico. Roche made 8 field goals and was 9 of 12 from the line, and his ball handling and ability to draw the fouls were the difference down the stretch.

In the 28 games of their sophomore season and first 8 games of 1969-70, either Roche or high school teammate Tom Owens had been South Carolina's leading scorer. The 37th time around, there was a new kid on the block.

"Tom Riker, a 6-10 happy-go-lucky sophomore from all places, Hicksville, N. Y., had to go and spoil things here Tuesday night in the championship game of the annual Sugar Bowl Tournament," sports editor Walt Riddle reported in *The Columbia Record.*

"The South Carolina center broke up this thing that John Roche and Tom Owens, teammates at LaSalle Academy in New York City, have had going since they joined the varsity ranks last year."

Riddle went on to say, "Riker, who like a good bottle of wine gets better with aging, ripped the cords at Loyola Field House for 36 points, 25 of which came in the first half, to spearhead the Gamecocks, ranked third nationally, to the Sugar Bowl Tournament championship..."

Riddle said Riker, who had played two exceptional games against Maryland and Long Island before Christmas but had "looked very ragged" in the win over New Mexico, "hit on 15 of 21 from the floor and 6 of 7 from the free throw line. He also picked up eight rebounds."

Riker's 25 first half points enabled South Carolina to hold a 41-34 lead at intermission. Roche had nine points at halftime.

Riker's first half play, according to Riddle, "forced Notre Dame to make several defensive changes in the second half and this opened things up for teammates Roche and Owens. Owens, who had only 2 points at halftime, finished with 13 and claimed 14 rebounds.

The Gamecock team watched most of the Notre Dame-West Virginia game the night before, and Riker credited personal observation of the Irish with helping his performance.

"It was great getting to see Notre Dame play Monday night against West Virginia ," the Gamecock sophomore said. It would be great to be able to do this all the time. This enables you to see for yourself how tough the man you have to guard is and you can look for things that you might be able to do against him."

Riker said his second half scoring dropped because Sid Catlett of Notre Dame "did a great job on me." But, he noted, "Roche pulled the game out for us in overtime," adding, "I gained a lot of confidence as the first half went along and confidence is the name of the game."

Riker and Roche, along with Carr, West Virginia's Will Robinson, and John Simogyi of New Mexico were named to the all-tournament team.

Bob Lipper, in a *Charlotte Observer* column, called Riker the Gamecocks' "screwball in residence," with a "loping walk and an impish grin."

Lipper said the whole town of Columbia was crazy, "even Frank McGuire, who is crazy like a fox. He is coach of the university's basketball team, you know, and in that capacity he is responsible for the well being of a rather large, somewhat goofy and highly talented piece of property named Tom Riker, who stands a mere 6-10 and will disappoint a lot of people if he doesn't play in at least two national championship teams before he is through."

The veteran John Roche said the sophomore Riker was "unbelievably enthusiastic" about basketball. "Like when we're eating," Roche related, "You'll take a look at him and he'll be taking a hook shot at the dinner table."

The extremely near sighted Riker, who wore horn rimmed glasses off the court and squinted through contact lenses in games, conceded, "I'm funny looking. Only the idiots laugh, but I probably do look funny on the court."

XII

South Carolina

vs

North Carolina

January 5, 1970--South Carolina 65, North Carolina 52

at Columbia

Six days after outlasting Notre Dame by one point in overtime to win the Sugar Bowl Classic in New Orleans, South Carolina opened the 1970 segment of its 1969-70 basketball season in Carolina Coliseum against the defending Atlantic Coast Conference Champion North Carolina Tar Heels.

The Gamecocks maintained their third ranking in the national polls on the strength of an 8-1 record and a seven game win streak. North Carolina was just one spot behind, ranked fourth.

North Carolina brought a 9-1 record to Columbia and matched the Gamecocks Sugar Bowl tournament title with the championship of the Carolina Classic in Greensboro, although the field wasn't as strong as faced by the Gamecocks in New Orleans. North Carolina defeated Harvard 92-74, and Bowling Green 89-72, to take the title in Greensboro.

In the championship game, Charlie Scott led North Carolina with 27 points and was named tournament MVP. North Carolina's only loss in its first ten games was to Kentucky, 94-87, at Charlotte.

Both teams had met Atlantic Coast Conference opponents in December. North Carolina was 1-0 in the league with an 80-76 win at Virginia, and South Carolina was 2-0 with victories over Virginia 62-51, and Maryland 101-68, both on the road.

The *Charlotte Observer* billed the matchup as "a battle for a share of the Atlantic Coast Conference lead and national ranking."

The newspaper sought to pin down Maryland coach Lefty Driesell and Virginia coach Bill Gibson on which was the better team. Both "tried to duck the question," but when pinned down, Driesell, who had played only the Gamecocks up to that point, picked South Carolina while Gibson, who had lost to both, picked North Carolina.

"South Carolina is by far the best team," Driesell was quoted, while Gibson said the Tar Heels were the better of the two because "North Carolina has more flexibility."

The *Observer* said "it will be hard for either coach to fool the other tonight. Dean Smith, coach of the Tar Heels, was an assistant to Frank McGuire, South Carolina coach, when he was at Chapel Hill. The two are old and close friends and have spent a lot of time talking basketball with each other."

The newspaper added both coaches were trying to "psyche" the other team, saying McGuire "contends that as the defending champions, North Carolina must be ranked as the favorite until someone beats them," while Smith was quoted as saying South Carolina "may be the best team in the nation right now."

An overflow crowd of 12,619 witnessed a slow paced first half as the two heavyweights felt each other out and North Carolina opened in its four corners stall offense. South Carolina went to the locker room with a 23-16 lead.

Dean Smith had predicted the slow pace in a pre-game interview, saying "we may have to go to the four corner offense a little earlier than we've done before."

Sports writer John Phelps referred to the four corners as "the Tar Heels' famed slowdown non-attack normally reserved for stalling out a slim lead in the closing moments of a game."

Few observers thought Smith "would employ the ball control tactics quite as early as he did last night," Phelps wrote in the Raleigh *News & Observer.*

"Before a packed house of booing, catcalling fans in Carolina Coliseum, the nationally No. 4-ranked Tar Heels unveiled the slowdown at the very beginning of their battle with No. 3-ranked South Carolina.

"A rash of second half fouls rendered the invaders' strategy ineffective, and the Gamecocks finally pulled away to a 65-52 triumph after holding only a 23-16 lead at intermission."

Phelps said Smith's strategy came within "6 feet and 8 inches" of working.

"The difference was a husky, 6-foot-8, piston-legged South Carolina forward named John Ribock. And if there were any Gamecock fans wondering what an Augusta, Ga., boy was doing in an otherwise all New York lineup for Frank McGuire's team, they found out last night right along with Smith and the Tar Heels."

Ribock had a sub-par 30.8 shooting percentage in South Carolina's first nine games, and Phelps said "Smith, naturally, elected to let Ribock take all the shots he wanted, trying in the meantime to bottle up the other Gamecocks."

Ribock responded by hitting six of nine field goal attempts in the first half, the only player on either team to score more than one basket in the first 20 minutes.

Phelps quoted John Roche as saying in a post game interview, "Usually I can tell when a player's really psyched up just by looking in his eyes. But, I guess everyone out there could see how psyched up Ribock was. You didn't have to look in his eyes."

McGuire said Ribock "was due for a night like that. He did so well last year, it had to come sometime."

Ribock added only one second half field goal, finishing with 14 points to lead the Gamecocks. Roche scored only two field goals but was 8-11 from the foul line for 12, as he controlled the basketball to protect the Gamecock lead down the stretch. Tom Owens had only one field goal but was 6-7 from the foul line.

A 9-0 run by South Carolina midway through the second half opened up a 12 point lead, 46-34. Charlie Scott hit two outside shots and Dennis Wuycik a layup to cut the margin to eight points at 51-43 with less than five minutes remaining.

"Roche took control of the ball in a frenzied in and out dribbling exhibition," John Phelps wrote, "designed to do exactly what it did...give the Gamecocks enough one and one free shot situations to pull away comfortably."

After defeating the Tar Heels, South Carolina stretched its winning streak to seventeen games before coming a cropper, 68-62, to Davidson on the Gamecocks' home floor. After the North Carolina game South Carolina defeated Maryland, Virginia, Furman, Clemson, Virginia Tech, Duke, Temple, Clemson again, and Wake Forest before losing to the Wildcats.

South Carolina closed out the season with five straight wins, defeating Duke, North Carolina State, North Carolina by 17 points at Chapel Hill, Wake Forest and North Carolina State at second time.

Only the first N. C. State game, a 71-69 victory at Raleigh, was close. Coach McGuire missed that contest, staying home with the influenza while assistant Donnie Walsh directed the Gamecocks from the bench.

Entering the Atlantic Coast Conference tournament at Charlotte with a 23-2 record, 14-0 in the conference, South Carolina was the top seed and the favorite to win the title and the ACC's bid to the NCAA playoffs. NCAA rules at that time allowed only one team from each conference in the national championship tournament.

Clemson, in last place, had fired Coach Bobby Roberts effective after the Tigers' season end, and Clemson, seeded eighth, had to play the Gamecocks in the ACC tournament's opening round. South Carolina had won the two regular season meetings by wide margins, 97-76 at Clemson and 99-52 at Columbia.

Roberts was determined not to end his career by letting the Gamecocks score in the 90s again so he had his team go into a deep freeze stall. There was no shot clock in 1970.

South Carolina held a one point lead, 34-33, but Clemson had the ball and a very good outside shooter in Butch Zatezalo with seconds to play. As Zatezalo dribbled to the left wing looking for the shot, Bobby Cremins stripped him of the basketball, and dribbled out of harms way as the game ended.

South Carolina had bitten the bullet and was in the semi-finals with a 24-2 record.

Wake Forest was next and the Gamecocks easily downed the Deacons, 79-63, but disaster struck in the form of a serious injury to John Roche with about three minutes left in the game.

Driving in for a layup, Roche stepped on the right foot of Wake Forest defender John Lewkowicz and went crashing to the floor. He suffered severe ligament damage to his left ankle. Roche attempted to play in the finals the following night against N.C. State, but was severely hobbled and the Wolfpack adopted Clemson's strategy by slowing the pace to a stall.

N.C. State won in two overtimes, 42-39, and as tournament champion represented the Atlantic Coast Conference in the NCAA East Regional.

For the second year in a row Roche was voted the ACC's Player of the Year and was named to several All-America teams.

Ironically, South Carolina was the regional host that year and as such was banned from accepting a bid to the National Invitation Tournament in New York City's Madison Square Garden.

The greatest team in Gamecock history finished with a 25-3 record but stayed home to watch St. Bonaventure, Villanova, Niagara and N.C. State battle it out in Carolina Coliseum. The Bonnies won the regional but lost All America center Bob Lanier to a knee injury in the title game against Villanova and wasn't able to win a game in the final four as UCLA cruised to another national championship.

XIII

South Carolina

vs

Notre Dame

December 5, 1970---South Carolina 85, Notre Dame 82

at South Bend, Indiana

John Roche's ankle healed over the summer and he and his Gamecock basketball team were the toast of the town and much of the nation entering the 1970-71 season.

Harry Lloyd, writing in *The Charlotte Observer*, said the room Roche and teammate Tom Owens shared in The Roost, South Carolina's residence hall for student-athletes, gave little indication that the two were basketball players.

"The pictures on the wall suggest an addiction to rock music rather than sports," Lloyd wrote. "There are no trophies visible, no nylon nets clipped from a goal in a distant coliseum. John Roche wears his fame modestly. He leads quietly, but there is no mistaking his leadership."

Lloyd added that Roche "realizes his importance to the South Carolina basketball team, and yet he can talk detachedly about himself and his relations to it. He neither overstates or underplays his role."

Steve Guback, assessing South Carolina in *The Sporting News*, wrote, "There hasn't been a club in this section of Dixie with as much potential since North Carolina won the national championship in 1957 and posted a flawless 32-0 mark. That Tar Heel team was coached by the same Mr. McGuire who does get around."

Guback added "There's talk that South Carolina, with four starters back from last season's 25-3 team, plus some gee whiz sophs, could be the No. 1 team in the republic, UCLA and its four straight NCAA championships notwithstanding."

Mike Martin, in a pre-season story in the Vailsburg, N. J., *Leader*, picked South Carolina to unseat UCLA as NCAA champion

"I'm picking South Carolina to edge out the Bruins for first place," Martin wrote, noting the Gamecocks' 25-3 record the previous year.

He also used the occasion to lamblast the Atlantic Coast Conference for picking the post season tournament champion rather than the regular season champion for the NCAA bid.

"I say they should abolish such playoffs with the exception of a tie at the end of the regular season," Martin declared. In 1970, only the ACC and the Southern Conference held post-season tournaments. Twenty five years later, most major conferences were holding tournaments at season end to cash in on the extra marketing and television opportunities.

While he bragged on South Carolina's strong lineup, Martin didn't pick any Gamecocks on his pre-season All-America team, relegating Roche to the second team and center Tom Riker to the third.

Sports Illustrated, in its pre-season rankings tabbed South Carolina second behind UCLA. *Basketball Extra, Basketball Weekly* and *Basketball News* also ranked the Gamecocks second. The Associated Press also ranked South Carolina second and picked Notre Dame fifth.

While two time captain and team leader Bobby Cremins was gone, Roche, Owens, John Ribock, Rick Aydlett and Bob Carver were back, joined by two highly regarded sophomores, 6-3 guard Kevin Joyce from New York's Archbishop Molloy High School and South Carolina's first seven footer, Danny Traylor, from Winston-Salem, N. C.

After opening with a routine, 84-63, home court win over Auburn, the Gamecocks traveled to South Bend, Ind., for a rematch with Notre Dame. The Irish still had super star Austin Carr and were still smarting from the one point overtime loss to the Gamecocks in New Orleans the previous December.

The result was a classic. Roche scored 32 points, including an incredible 16 of 16 from the foul line. Carr scored 27 and four other Irish players were in double figures. Tom Riker scored 22 for South Carolina, Tom Owens had 15 and sophomore Kevin Joyce, in his second varsity game, contributed 13.

When the smoke cleared, South Carolina prevailed 85-82 in a game that was as much a classic as was the showdown in the Sugar Bowl tournament finals in New Orleans a year earlier, and for the second time in a row the Gamecocks won.

Coach Frank McGuire opened with a man-to-man defense but quickly switched to a zone in an effort to deny Carr the ball. The strategy was also to minimize fouling by the Gamecocks who built a ten point halftime lead, 45-35.

Notre Dame charged out in the second half to tie the game at 56-56 with 10:32 left, and then 58-58. Tom Riker's three point play put South Carolina back on top to stay, but the nail biting wasn't over.

With eight minutes and twelve seconds left in the game, Notre Dame cut South Carolina's lead to two points, 64-62, and the 11,343 fans in attendance were in a frenzy.

Roche quieted the crowd with 7:19 remaining by sinking a twenty footer and was fouled after the shot. He made both ends of the one and one and the four point play boosted the lead to six points. In the final 5 minutes and 16 seconds Roche added 14 points, 10 of them from the foul line as the Gamecocks broke the Irish press and paraded to the foul line.

South Carolina led by eight, 81-73, with 2:03 to go and held on to win by three points.

"I'm glad to win by even one point here," McGuire said in his post game interview, at the same time heaping praise on two All-America players, his own John Roche and Notre Dame's Austin Carr.

"Carr is tremendous," McGuire enthused. "That boy can really carry a team and make the big play. We had him in the position several times tonight when I hoped he would take the shot. He did just that and they kept going through the hoop."

McGuire said, "Our zone defense plus John Roche's play were the keys to the victory. We started out in a man-to-man defense, but switched to a zone to shut off Carr. And it worked as he got just two baskets from the floor in the first half and had only three shots."

Notre Dame Coach Johnny Dee's analysis of the game was "Old Frank just outfoxed me for a second and it got our team in trouble from the start. I actually thought he would come out in a man-to-man and put Roche on Austin. We did it and put Austin on John."

Dan Foster of the Greenville *News* noted that Tom Owens was also tremendous for South Carolina, especially in the first half.

"Tom Owens was superb..." Foster wrote. "He dominated the Notre Dame board and scored 13 points himself, 10 of them in the first 11 minutes." Owens scored 2 in the second half to finish with 15.

Foster said Roche not only scored fourteen first half points but he "set Owens up for some four footers."

Carr had only six points at halftime and Foster noted South Carolina's 2-3 zone "seemed to hurt him." However, the Irish All-America scored 21 after intermission.

Jim Huber of the Spartanburg *Herald-Journal* said South Carolina, "in a driving snowstorm and sub-freezing weather...notched a hard fought, intelligently played 85-82 victory over the fifth ranked Irish of Notre Dame."

Herman Helms of Columbia's *The State*, wrote "South Carolina's Gamecocks won that big, critical early season game they wanted and needed so badly, clipping powerful Notre Dame..."

Helms added the Gamecocks won because "they made use of their physical assets and commanding board play."

And, he added, "they won because they held the Irish's All-American Austin Carr to just a good game, not the fantastic game for which he is noted. They won because John Roche didn't play just a good game. He played his usual great one."

A Monday story in *The Columbia Record*, an afternoon newspaper, by sports editor Walt Riddle said "John Roche truly put on his most fantastic and pressure packed performance of his three year varsity career. Sure, he has had better games as far as shooting percentage goes, but never against a tougher foe."

Roche, who had nine assists to go with his 32 points, wasn't completely satisfied with his performance. While he made all 16 of his free throw attempts he was 8 for 20 from field goal range.

"I'm just not shooting like I ought to," he remarked on the charter plane ride home. " He added, "We could have broken the game open if I had hit some of those easy shots I had."

While he preferred the fast break attack to the controlled type offense, Roche told Riddle "A team can't make the mistake of doing what the opposition likes best. Notre Dame only knows how to run and shoot, while we can do either. I feel we are the only team in the country who can win at both."

XIV

South Carolina

vs

Western Kentucky

Dec. 30, 1970--South Carolina 86, Western Kentucky 84 (Holiday Festival Championship)

at New York City

South Carolina took a 5-0 record to New York City's Madison Square Garden in late December 1970 to compete in the Eastern Collegiate Athletic Association's Holiday Festival.

After opening at home with an easy win over Auburn and edging Notre Dame 85-82 at South Bend, Ind., the Gamecocks drubbed Duke 98-78 and Maryland 96-70 at home before surviving a scare at Blacksburg, Va. Tom Riker's tip in with one second remaining provided a 78-76 come from behind win over Virginia Tech.

Riker's tip concluded an uphill climb for the Gamecocks who trailed by nine points midway through the second half.

The win over Maryland didn't go the full forty minutes. With the second ranked Gamecocks ahead by twenty six points, a wild fight broke out and officials terminated the game with 4:52 left on the clock.

Films of the game indicated Maryland's Darrell Brown punched South Carolina's Rick Aydlett in the scuffle for the rebound off a missed free throw. Aydlett retaliated and both benches emptied with Coach Lefty Driesell leading the charge off the Maryland bench.

Before order was restored, Gamecock strong man John Ribock had landed a couple of haymakers on Driesell, prompting Lefty to threaten legal action. Referee George Conley declared the game over with the score standing pending review by the Atlantic Coast Conference Commissioner's office.

Dr. Thomas F. Jones, University of South Carolina president, telegraphed an apology and regrets to Maryland president Wilson H. Elkins. Jones said the incident was "deeply regretted by all of us at the University of South Carolina."

After studying reports on the melee for a week, acting ACC Commissioner Norvall Neve absolved South Carolina of any negligence in the incident, but he warned that the next game between the two schools might have to be played at a neutral site.

It wasn't. South Carolina faced a Maryland slowdown and a hostile crowd, Jan. 9, at College Park with Maryland upsetting the Gamecocks in overtime, 31-30. They would meet a third time in the ACC tournament at Greensboro with South Carolina winning 71-63.

But, back to Madison Square Garden and the Holiday Festival.

In the opening round, South Carolina rolled over Cornell 83-60 with John Roche scoring 28 points and Tom Riker contributing 21. However, the next morning forward Tom Owens was hospitalized with an intestinal virus and would be unavailable for the semi-final game against Providence.

One New York sportswriter wasn't impressed with South Carolina or co-favorite, fifth ranked Western Kentucky, and the first round of the Holiday Festival.

"Underwhelming South Carolina, under-achieving Western Kentucky, under-sized Providence and inexperienced St. John's battle for the Holiday Festival finals berths," Maury Allen wrote in the New York *Post.* Allen said South Carolina impressed nobody in defeating Cornell and Western Kentucky was pushed to "nervous exhaustion" by St. Peter's.

Western Kentucky, led by seven footer Jim McDaniels, outscored St. Peter's 108-97, and reached the finals with an 86-67 win over St. John's. In the two games, McDaniels scored 63 points, the same number accrued by South Carolina's Roche in the tournament's first two rounds.

Without the 6-10 Owens, and using only six players against Providence, Coach Frank McGuire's team passed the century mark to win 102-86. Both Roche and Riker topped 30, Roche scoring 35 points and Riker adding 31. Kevin Joyce, who moved from guard to Owens' forward spot, although he was seven inches shorter than tall Tom, contributed 21, as three players accounted for 87 of South Carolina's 102 points.

Bob Carver started in Joyce's guard spot and scored eight points while forward John Ribock scored five and Rick Aydlett had two off the bench.

Riker also had nineteen rebounds.

In the second half, South Carolina shot 64.7 per cent, making 22 of 34 field goal attempts. From the foul line, the Gamecocks made 26 of 31. They led 46-33 at halftime and never looked back.

St. John's coach Frank Mulzoff called the South Carolina-Western Kentucky matchup a tossup, but hedged by expressing a preference for the Gamecocks, coached by his mentor Frank McGuire.

John Ribock (41) blocks a shot to help South Carolina defeat Western Kentucky in the championship game of the 1970 Holiday Festival in New York City's Madison Square Garden.—*USC Sports Information*

"Do you want my choice? I'd say its a tossup," Mulzoff told reporters. "But, you know my sentimental choice."

One of Mulzoff's players, Mel Davis, disagreed with his coach, saying, "Western Kentucky will win. They are too fast and two strong for them."

Holy Cross coach Jack Donohue, whose team didn't meet South Carolina in the tournament, said he didn't think anyone could beat the Gamecocks.

"They just have everything," he said.

Maury Allen predicted the stars of the two teams, South Carolina's Roche and Western Kentucky's McDaniels, "will not only settle the Festival title by their performances...but individual honors. The MVP winner will be one of these two if there are no upsets."

New York *Daily News* writer Phil Pepe, alluding to the large number of New Yorkers on Coach Frank McGuire's roster, wrote "South Carolina will be the only New York team in the finals of the 19th annual ECAC Holiday Festival," noting that Western Kentucky's "tall, talented and fifth-ranked Hilltoppers spoiled the chances of an all-New York final" by routing St. John's.

The championship game was a classic.

Jim Huber, writing in the Spartanburg *Herald-Journal*, said "It was a game that might be played over and over again for the pure basketball fan. McDaniels was magnificent, winning the Most Valuable Player award for his awesome play."

McDaniels scored 26 points and claimed 12 rebounds, but South Carolina won the game, withstanding a Hilltopper charge in the waning moments that fell just short.

South Carolina held a six point lead, 86-80, after John Roche converted two one and one foul opportunities with 47 and 19 seconds remaining. Jim Rose hit a 20 footer for Western Kentucky and Rex Bailey stole the inbounds pass and scored a layup with six seconds left. Western Kentucky called a time out.

The Gamecocks successfully got the ball in bounds, but Jimmy Dunn stole it and passed off to McDaniels. He took a dribble before shooting and the horn ending the game sounded a split second before McDaniels released the basketball, which banked off the backboard into the basket.

The tying goal was waved off and the South Carolina Gamecocks were the champions of the Holiday Festival before a near capacity crowd of 18,243 in Madison Square Garden.

South Carolina built a seven point halftime lead, 45-38, and led most of the game, but the Gamecocks were unable to put the Hilltoppers away. Accuracy at the foul line again bailed South Carolina out, the Gamecocks making 26 of 31 while Western Kentucky converted only 6 of 13.

Although held to 14 points after scoring 63 in the first two games, Roche made 6 of 7 free throw tries, including 4 points on the pair of one and ones in the final minute. Whenever the Gamecocks went to the wire trying to protect a lead, McGuire always wanted the ball in the hands of his best foul shooter.

However, the most impressive foul shooter in the game was 6-10 center Tom Riker. He converted 10 of 10 and finished with 24 points. Sophomore Kevin Joyce was the Gamecocks' leading scorer with 25. He made 11 of 16 field goal attempts and 3 of 4 free throws.

"Kevin is really something," said Tom Owens, who returned to the lineup following his hospitalization and scored 17 points. He also led all rebounders with 14.

"His shooting is so great," Owens said of Joyce. It's really a joke. Before the game he was walking around saying how we were going to beat Western Kentucky. I don't think he knows what pressure is."

Owens said he couldn't understand McDaniels being named MVP over one of the Gamecocks.

"I thought Riker or Joyce should have gotten it," he said.

Roche also praised Riker and Joyce, saying, "I didn't play a good game. Riker and Joyce were the ones that pulled us through."

"One point is worth a million to me," Coach Frank McGuire said in his post-game comments. "I'm proud of this victory. We beat a fine ball club, one of the best we've played."

McGuire had praise for McDaniels, saying "He's a pro already. He made one stuff shot over his head that I still don't believe."

McGuire's comment about McDaniels being "a pro already" may have beeen truer that he realized. The Hilltoppers went on to the final four and the championship game, but the NCAA later vacated the second place finish because McDaniels had had improper dealings with a professional agent.

"Undefeated South Carolina and previously undefeated Western Kentucky waged a magnificent basketball struggle," was the way Gordon S. White, Jr., described the game in the *New York Times.*

"The struggle between two excellently balanced teams finished with the most thrilling last few seconds seen in a college game at the Garden in many years," White wrote.

Executive sports editor Herman Helms of Columbia's *The State,* called it "a classic basketball game with a heartstopper finish."

Helms pointed out South Carolina had won the Quaker City Classic and the Sugar Bowl tournaments the two previous seasons, "and there were many good reasons why they made it three in a row."

Western Kentucky Coach John Oldham said, "If there was any one key to South Carolina's victory, I would have to say it was Joyce's shooting from the outside. That really hurt us.

Bob Cole of *The State* said the final seconds were "too unreal to be anything but fiction."

South Carolina would stretch its unbeaten streak to nine games with an easy win over Clemson before losing at North Carolina. The Gamecocks would compile a 20-4 regular season record before making school history in the ACC tournament.

XV

South Carolina

vs

North Carolina

Feb. 20, 1971--South Carolina 72, North Carolina 66

at Columbia

Following the win over Western Kentucky in the championship game of the Holiday Festival in Madison Square Garden, Dec. 30, 1970, South Carolina's fortunes took a roller coaster ride during the month of January in 1971.

The Gamecocks whipped Clemson the second day of the New Year to improve their record to 9-0, but lost by 15 points at Chapel Hill two nights later, 79-64. An 84-71 home court win over Temple was tempered by a disastrous road trip to Maryland and Virginia.

A Dec. 16, 1970 game with Maryland in Carolina Coliseum, which South Carolina easily won, 96-70, ended in an on court brawl and referee George Conley ended the game with four minutes and fifty two seconds showing on the clock. Maryland coach Lefty Driesell threatened legal action against South Carolina's John Ribock. Driesell led the charge off the Maryland bench and was the recipient of a couple of punches thrown by Ribock.

The legal action never materialized but the Terrapins were loaded for bear when the Gamecocks arrived in College Park.

Maryland students dressed in armor as Roman warriors ringed the Cole Field House court. Driesell ordered his team to stall and the score was 4-3 in Maryland's favor at the half. John Roche made a free throw and Kevin Joyce a 15 foot jumper with 7:51 left in the half. South Carolina's only other shot was a miss by Tom Riker.

The regulation forty minutes ended with the score tied at 25-25. South Carolina scored the first five points of the overtime to lead 30-25, but Maryland got a basket, a steal and a basket to cut it to 30-29, and another steal and a basket in the dying seconds to win 31-30 in a major upset.

After that crushing Saturday night loss, McGuire and the Gamecocks had the weekend to fret before meeting Virginia Monday night in Charlottesville. Cavalier star Barry Parkhill's miracle long range basket at the buzzer dealt South Carolina its second consecutive crushing defeat, 50-49.

A Virginia fan poured a soft drink on South Carolina assistant athletics director Ralph Floyd as he and I were attempting to escort Coach McGuire from the court to post-game interviews. Nearby security guards snickered but took no action to intervene. Such conduct was the order of the day in the super competitive Atlantic Coast Conference, and we were not totally innocent at South Carolina.

A group of law students who managed to obtain seats behind the visitor's radio broadcast position on press row in Carolina Coliseum would often shout obscenities into the microphones. I stationed my seat next to the visitor's radio in an effort to prevent such behavior and was threatened with a lawsuit by a student who was escorted out of the building by security after being heard throughout the Tar Heel Network during a game with North Carolina.

In the old Fike Field House at Clemson, football players sat behind the baskets and once gave South Carolina player Frank Standard a sound pummeling when he fell into the stands chasing a loose ball. Frank McGuire often complained about the conduct of Clemson fans behind the visitor's bench in Littlejohn Coliseum.

Wake Forest students once threw a live chicken into the midst of South Carolina's pre-game huddle. The frightened bird defecated on the floor and the mess wasn't noticed until one of the game officials stepped in and nearly fell down.

In another incident at Wake Forest, the Demon Deacon mascot and cheerleaders hauled a toilet onto the court and stuffed an effigy of John Roche into it, the mascot tamping the effigy down with his toilet plunger baton.

With a 10-3 record, the Gamecocks took a 19 day break for final exams and had a long time to think things over. In a rematch on Jan. 30, they clobbered Virginia by 22 points, 92-70, in Carolina Coliseum. They started February with an 82-71 road loss at Duke, but wouldn't lose again until the NCAA playoffs.

The February surge included an 118-83 rout of Furman in the coliseum, Feb. 4, in which John Roche scored a school record 56 points. I can claim some responsibility for the record. Coach McGuire had taken his starters out when I informed him that John had 52 points and the record was 54, set by Grady Wallace Dec. 21, 1956 in a 96-81 win over Georgia at Athens.

McGuire sent Roche back in and he quickly made two field goals to eclipse Wallace's record by two points. Fifty six points remained the school single season record through the 1995 season.

Midway through a twelve game win streak, Feb. 20, 1971, South

Carolina lined up against Dean Smith's North Carolina Tar Heels in the coliseum, seeking to avenge the Jan. 4 loss at Chapel Hill.

Sports Editor Doug Nye of *The Columbia Record*, described the result in these words:

"North Carolina actually started it all, and Saturday afternoon the Tar Heels had to suffer for it.

"Back in early January UNC Coach Dean Smith decided his team would not play against South Carolina's highly-touted zone defense. Instead, he would force the Gamecocks to play man-to-man.

"The move produced a Tar Heel victory and also gave other ACC teams, like Maryland and Virginia, food for thought. That made things rough for the Gamecocks for awhile, but as the season wore on South Carolina became more and more polished at the man-to-man style of play.

"N.C. State found out just how polished last Wednesday night (79-63 South Carolina with Roche contributing 41 points) and North Carolina discovered likewise Saturday afternoon in Carolina Coliseum

"Hustling at a near-frenzied pace, Coach Frank McGuire's crew rode a great defensive effort to an important 72-66 conquest of the Tar Heels before an excited crowd of 12,717."

Nye's game story went on to say it was "another stupendous offensive showing" by All-America John Roche, who scored 32 points, but, Nye added, the Gamecocks' senior captain was obviously prouder of the team's defensive performance.

"Our defense was the key, especially in the first half," Roche told reporters in a post game interview. "We didn't want to let them get the easy shot. We've just been trying to be more aggressive in recent games."

The South Carolina defense was so aggressive that North Carolina managed only 3 field goals in the first half but converted 20 free throws and South Carolina led by 12 points, 38-26, at intermission.

"Although the Tar Heels had their problems from the floor," Nye opined, "they used some rather accurate free throw shooting to stay in the foul plagued game.

The two teams combined committed 57 personal fouls and 66 free throws were made, 36 by North Carolina and 30 by South Carolina. That shattered the coliseum record of 53 total fouls and 62 free throws made set just three days earlier in the game with N. C. State.

South Carolina made 21 of 40 field goal attempts, 52.5 per cent and the Tar Heels made only 15 of 41 for 36.6 per cent.

Dennis Wuycik led North Carolina with 21 points, Bill Chamberlain had 17 and George Karl 16. Lee Dedmon, North Carolina's 6-10 center, scored only 6, all from the foul line and no other Tar Heel had more than 4. Besides Roche, the only Gamecock in double figures was Tom Owens with 14.

North Carolina spent most of the second half chipping away at the Gamecock lead, creeping to within 3 at 54-51 with 4:19 remaining. South Carolina spurted back to an 11 point advantage, 64-53, with 1:50 remaining but half a minute later, North Carolina was back within 4 at 64-60. The Tar Heels never got closer, and the final margin was 6 points to improve South Carolina's record to 16-4.

Roche made 14 of 16 free throws and 9 of 15 field goal attempts, leading Nye to write, "Roche has been so super this month (34 points per game) no one would be surprised if it was discovered he put on his uniform in a telephone booth."

Roche felt he had a couple of games "where I was off in my shooting."

However, he added, "Of course, when you make a few, you gain more confidence in your shooting."

In answer to a reporter's question, he replied, "Yes, I like that baseline shot a lot. Besides being a good shot, it draws fouls."

In assessing the win over the Tar Heels, Roche said "This was a big win for us, but I still think we blew a lot of opportunities to really put the game out of reach."

Teammate Bob Carver agreed: "We could have made this an easy game. When we get an 11 point lead or so, it seems we tend to let up just a little bit. But, when it gets down to 4 or 5, we always seem to come through with a key basket."

Carver credited the South Carolina football squad with contributing to the victory:

"We were up for this one. We could have been psyched up for it even if the stands had been empty. But, our great fans just help us even more, And the football players, man, they're something."

The football squad organized its own cheering section and formed two lines to greet the Gamecocks when they entered the court."

"Once the contest begins, their vocal support is quite evident," Doug Nye wrote.

After defeating North Carolina, South Carolina drubbed Houston, which brought an 18-4 record to Carolina Coliseum, 88-71, Wake Forest, 84-64, N. C. State at Raleigh, 82-69, and Wake Forest on the road, 88-73, to take a 20-4 record and a nine game win streak into the Atlantic Coast Conference Tournament at Greensboro.

Roche scored only 14 points in the win over Houston as the Cougars triple teamed him, leaving other Gamecocks open. The 14 points were low among five Gamecocks. Tom Owens led with 19 points and raked in an incredible 26 rebounds. Tom Riker and Rick Aydlett scored 16 each and Bob Carver had 15. The game was twelve and a half minutes old before Roche attempted his first field goal.

Beauty queen Vickie Chesser covered the Houston game as a sidebar writer for *The Columbia Record*, and asked Roche about his low scoring total.

"What makes us so great is that one guy is just as good as the other," he replied. "We aren't a one man team."

During halftime of the home win over Wake Forest, the final home game of his great career, the jersey number 11 worn by Roche was officially retired. Only one other South Carolina basketball number, the 42 worn by Grady Wallace, had been retired up to that point.

With the Gamecocks winning easily, by 20 points, Roche took few shots in his final home game. He scored 12 points and dealt out 7 assists. Wake Forest's Charlie Davis, who would deny Roche his third consecutive ACC Player of the Year Award, scored 16 points in the first half but was limited to 4 after intermission, finishing with 20, 7 points below his average.

"Davis had a good first half," Roche said, "but our zone stopped him in the second half. Davis is a great ball player. We feel if we can hold him to his average or below then we've done a good job. Even if we hold him to 30 or 35 points and stop the rest of them we know we can win."

"John is a magician with the ball," Frank McGuire said. "There are so many things he does and all of them perfectly. He's one of the finest players I've ever coached."

When asked by a reporter on the eve of the ACC tournament, Roche replied, "To tell the truth, it doesn't matter to us where we're seeded for the tournament. We're just looking forward to it."

XVI

South Carolina

vs

North Carolina

March 13, 1971--South Carolina 52, North Carolina 51 (Atlantic Coast Conference Tournament Championship)

at Greensboro, North Carolina

Shortly before he took his team to Greensboro for what would be South Carolina's last participation as a member of the Atlantic Coast Conference, Frank McGuire was named one of the ten best groomed men in the United States by *Men's Hairstylist and Barber's Journal*, the leading publication of the barbering and men's hair-styling industry.

McGuire recalled it was the second time he had made the top ten. He was on the 1958 list along with then U. S. Vice President Richard Nixon.

North Carolina had ended regular season play in first place in the ACC with South Carolina a close second. The two Carolinas had split during the season, each winning on its home floor, and it seemed destined the Gamecocks and Tar Heels should meet in the tournament finals with the winner of the rubber game establishing superiority and earning the ACC's automatic bid to the NCAA playoffs.

The intensity of the rivalry spilled over to some of the fans and sports editor Smith Barrier of the Greensboro *Daily News* published, without comment from himself, a number of letters from Tar Heels supporters still reeling from the 72-66 North Carolina loss at Columbia.

Robert D. Walker of Biscoe, N.C., took the two announcers on the ACC telecast to task for what he perceived as biased reporting favoring South Carolina: "...It's pretty bad when a fan has to turn off the sound of Jim Thacker and Bobby Roberts and switch to the sound of radio because of the comments of these announcers. In the game today the only name mentioned hardly at all was John Roche...but fans could hear no favorable comment for (North) Carolina. This same thing happens in every game..."

Another fan, Bill Anderson of Greensboro, blamed the officiating for the North Carolina loss, writing to Barrier, "The officiating was the worse I have ever seen."

He ignored the fact that North Carolina attempted 42 free throws in the game and South Carolina, fouled just as many times by the Tar Heels, also attempted 42.

Kenny Day of Liberty, N.C., wrote he had "never seen a dirtier game."

South Carolina, with its 20-4 regular season record, went into the ACC tournament ranked sixth nationally behind perennial NCAA champion UCLA, Marquette, Southern California, Pennsylvania and Kansas. North Carolina, 20-5, was thirteenth.

The Atlantic Coast Sports Writers Assn., announced its All-ACC team on the eve of the tournament and for the third consecutive year John Roche was on the first team. Teammate Tom Owens made the first unit for the second time. Roche received 119 of 121 votes cast. Charlie Davis of Wake Forest was the only unanimous choice. Others on the first team included junior Dennis Wuycik of North Carolina, the only non-senior chosen, and Randy Denton of Duke.

Sports Editor Bruce Phillips of the Raleigh *Times* marveled at the Gamecock prowess in a pre-tournament column:

"Now it looked familiar. It was all coming back. A lean, whippet with a long nose and hair flopping Byronically over his forehead would call for the basketball in the backcourt and dribble slowly up the floor.

"The other four members of the team would take their places near the goal and wait for their leader to launch the attack.

"He would cunningly move into his defender, catching him in a pick, searching until he found a screen, or passing off to a teammate left open by his threatening presence.

"When a shot was missed another was tried, and another until success was attained. At the other end of the court, five men banded to form an almost impregnable bulwark.

"After marinating for a month, the South Carolina basketball team has come to a quick boil. The Gamecocks are awesome again and with simple majesty.

"The Gamecocks have gone back to their old style of seek and destroy, and have proven beyond doubt in recent weeks that they are now the team to reckon with in the ACC, maybe the country."

Phillips said, "If John Roche sounds cocky, well, he is. But Roche fans will say, if you've got it, flaunt it. He can be, and often is, on the supernatural side."

Against N.C. State, Phillips pointed out, "Roche scored 37 points

—22 in the last half—had the Wolfpack cross-eyed and easily led South Carolina to an 82-69 romp."

The Raleigh sports editor added "Coaches are agreed that Roche can single-handedly masticate a defense."

South Carolina's plan, according to Roche, wrote Phillips, was the same as a year earlier when the top seeded Gamecocks—with Roche hobbled by an ankle injury—lost a double overtime championship game to N.C. State.

"We went into the tournament knowing we were the best team," Phillips quoted Roche. "We go into it this year knowing the same thing. We might be seeded second but that doesn't mean a thing."

The Sporting News announced its All-America team, naming John Roche of South Carolina along with Sidney Wicks of UCLA, Jim McDaniels of Western Kentucky, Artis Gilmore of Jacksonville, Austin Carr of Notre Dame, and a sixth player, Ken Durrett of LaSalle. Roche also was a first team All-America choice by the U. S. Basketball Writers; United Press International; Basketball Weekly; United Savings Helms Foundation; and the NBA Coaches. He was named to the second team by The Associated Press and the National Association of Basketball Coaches.

Roche became only the third ACC player to make major All-America basketball teams for three consecutive years. The others were Art Heyman of Duke (1961-63) and Lennie Rosenbluth of North Carolina (1955-57)

While it wouldn't become official until several weeks after the tournament, there were growing indications that South Carolina would withdraw from the Atlantic Coast Conference to make its way as an independent, so the 1971 tournament at Greensboro was a swan song for the Gamecocks.

Bob Cole, assistant sports editor of *The State*, analyzed the strengths and weaknesses of the tournament field.

North Carolina's strengths, he said, were depth, effective pressing defense, and spectacularly effective shot selection. A weakness was lack of a truly big center who dominates the boards and competes effectively on defense.

Otherwise, Cole wrote, "The Tar Heels are sound."

South Carolina's strengths, as cited by Cole, were "One of the nation's finest take-charge guards in John Roche, excellent size and rebounding strength and a good bench that will be even stronger with the return of sophomore Kevin Joyce, idled by a leg operation."

Cole said South Carolina's weaknesses were "overall speed and quickness."

The Winston-Salem *Journal and Sentinel* stated there were two kinds of basketball fans in the Atlantic Coast Conference, "those who love South Carolina and those who hate South Carolina."

Since the tournament was being played in Greensboro, the Winston-Salem newspaper deduced, "the latter group is by far the largest"...and "the boos will outnumber the cheers" when the Gamecocks compete.

South Carolina and North Carolina were both businesslike in disposing of quarterfinal and semifinal opponents enroute to their inevitable showdown in the finals. The Gamecocks brushed aside Maryland 71-63 and N. C. State 69-56, while the Tar Heels toyed with Clemson, 76-41, and then disposed of Virginia, 78-68. Duke, the third seed, was eliminated in the first round, 68-61, by N. C. State, and Virginia reached the semis by edging Wake Forest 85-84.

Mel Derrick, sports director of the Winston-Salem *Journal and Sentinel,* called it "the dream final," adding, "the No. 1 seed vs. the No. 2 seed. The regular season king, North Carolina, vs. the nation's sixth ranked team, South Carolina."

Frank McGuire was quoted as saying, "It should be a great match, the rubber match. North Carolina beat us at North Carolina. We beat them at South Carolina. This is a game I'd like to watch myself."

From a standpoint of finesse, the championship game of the 1971 Atlantic Coast Conference basketball tournament was not well played. From a standpoint of excitement, the finish ranks near the top of the all time thrill department.

South Carolina shot a miserable 27.9 per cent from the field, making only 17 of 61 attempts. North Carolina shot a respectable 46.2 per cent but the Gamecock defense limited the Tar Heels to 39 tries and their 18 field goals were only one more than South Carolina's. The Gamecocks made 18 of 24 free throws, 75 per cent, to 15 of 28, 53.6 per cent and it was failure at the foul line in the waning minutes that doomed the Tar Heels.

That, and the leaping ability of six foot three inch South Carolina sophomore Kevin Joyce.

South Carolina also won the rebounding battle but just by a couple, 37-35.

Both teams appeared cautious and up tight in the early going and halftime found the Tar Heels clinging to a two point lead, 21-19. Executive Sports Editor Smith Barrier of the Greensboro *Daily News* said the halftime statistics "were like reading a funeral report," adding, "It had been 20 opening minutes of the thinking man's game."

South Carolina took its first lead, 25-24, two and a half minutes into the second half. The Gamecock sagging one-three-one zone defense limited North Carolina to fifteen second half shots, nine of them successful.

With five seconds remaining on the game clock, South Carolina's Tom Owens (24) lays the ball in the basket to give the Gamecocks a 52-51 win over North Carolina and the championship of the 1971 ACC tournament. Kevin Joyce, 6-3 (not shown) out jumped 6-10 Lee Dedmon of North Carolina to tap the ball to Owens.—*Larry Cagle, The State*

North Carolina led by seven points, 42-35, with six minutes left in the game. The lead was six, 46-40, at the 4:34 mark but three buckets by Roche, John Ribock and Tom Owens, tied it at 46-46. The clock showed 3:23.

A layup by Bill Chamberlain and a free throw by George Karl gave the Tar Heels a 3 point advantage, 49-46, with 1:19 to play. Roche cut it to 1 with a 17 foot jumper but Lee Dedmon made a free throw 1:04 from the end of regulation and it was 50-48. John Ribock's free throw at 0:45 cut it to 1 point.

Bob Carver stole a pass and fed Ribock, who was fouled. He made one of two and with 39 seconds left, it was tied at 50. Dedmon made the first of two free throws to give North Carolina a 51-50 lead with 18 seconds left but missed the second and Rick Aydlett rebounded for South Carolina.

The ball went to Kevin Joyce who started up the base line and collided with Dedmon. Gamecock fans expected a foul and a one and one opportunity. The officials, Steve Honzo and Ralph Stout, signaled jump ball. Under today's alternating possession rule circumstances would have been dramatically different.

Dean Smith called time out. There were six seconds left. North Carolina led 51-50. Joyce was six feet three. Dedmon was six feet ten. Smith instructed Dedmon to tip the ball toward George Karl, away from the South Carolina basket.

Afterward, Joyce said his instructions in the South Carolina huddle were to "jump to the moon."

The ball went up. Filmed replays showed Joyce's hand at the apex of his leap, several inches above Dedmon's, although some of the North Carolina writers reported that Dedmon accidentally tipped the basketball to Tom Owens.

Everyone but the jumpers and Owens, broke up court. Joyce tipped the basketball to a startled Owens who gently laid it in the basket as the clock showed three seconds to play.

North Carolina managed to get a time out with one second remaining. The 15,170 fans were both exhausted and stunned. The Tar Heels attempted a length of the court pass but it was intercepted and the game was over. South Carolina's fans were exuberant. North Carolina's were dismayed.

South Carolina 52, North Carolina 51. The Gamecocks were Atlantic Coast Conference Champions.

"I just missed it," is the way Dedmon explained Joyce controlling the jump ball. One North Carolina sports writer wasn't kind to the Tar Heels.

"Choke is a very strong word," wrote Robert Noell in the Winston-Salem *Journal and Sentinel*, "one despised more than any other by athletes. But there's no other word that can describe what happened to North Carolina.

"It wasn't Tom Owens and South Carolina who beat UNC. The Tar Heels accomplished the feat by themselves."

Roche and Dedmon tied for the Everett Case Award, given to the tournament's Most Valuable Player, as voted by the news media. Dedmon joined Gamecocks Roche and Owens on the All-Tournament team along with Barry Parkhill of Virginia and Paul Coder of N.C. State.

Roche led all scorers in the low scoring game with 18 points and Owens scored 14, including the most important two points of his career. Dennis Wuycik led North Carolina with 16, despite fouling out early. Karl had 13 and Dedmon 12.

In the media interview room Owens said "That's got to be the biggest shot I've ever made. I was in such a state of shock when I saw the ball coming toward me. I couldn't believe it. Once I got the ball I knew they weren't going to let me make it. I figured I would get clobbered going up, but there was no one around me."

Dean Smith rationalized the loss by saying, "We got a big lead too soon. With a six point lead we acted like we had it won and obviously we didn't."

"Better to be lucky than good," is the way Frank McGuire described the jump ball that produced the startling climax.

Five days after the miracle jump ball in Greensboro, the Gamecocks had to return to Tobacco Road to meet undefeated Pennsylvania in the NCAA East Regional tournament in Raleigh's Reynolds Coliseum. It was hostile territory with most of the fans from North Carolina.

Emotionally drained from the ACC tournament, the Gamecocks lost to the Quakers 79-64 and then lost the consolation game 100-90 to a Fordham team coached by a young Digger Phelps.

John Roche finished his collegiate career with a then school record 1,910 points and a 22.5 points per game average in 85 games. He compiled his total in three seasons and through 1995 had been surpassed only by Alex English, who came in under the freshman eligibility rule and scored 1,972 points in four seasons.

Tom Owens scored 1,325 career points in 84 games. He led the Atlantic Coast Conference in rebounding three consecutive seasons and finished with 1,116 career rebounds, through 1995 second only to the 1,159 rebounds by Lee Collins, who played four seasons from 1952-53 through 1955-56.

The Gamecocks bowed out as a member of the Atlantic Coast Conference with a 23-6 record for the 1970-71 season.

XVII

South Carolina

vs

Temple

March 11, 1972---South Carolina 53, Temple 51 (NCAA Tournament First Round)

at Williamsburg, Virginia

The John Roche--Tom Owens era was over as South Carolina prepared for the 1971-72 basketball season. So was the Gamecock membership in the Atlantic Coast Conference.

South Carolina's withdrawal from the ACC had become official in the summer of 1971 and the only Atlantic Coast Conference opponent on the 1971-72 schedule was in-state rival Clemson. South Carolina's first schedule as an independent looked as if the Gamecocks had joined the Catholic League.

Santa Clara, Villanova, Fairfield, Boston College, Marquette, Manhattan, St. Bonaventure, Niagara, Fordham, Notre Dame were some of the names that dotted the schedule as Coach Frank McGuire's friends came to his rescue in the face of the ACC boycott and McGuire put together a competitive schedule on short notice.

Roche, Owens and John Ribock had graduated but there were some familiar names remaining on the roster. Tom Riker, Rick Aydlett and Bob Carver were seniors. Kevin Joyce, the hero of the miracle jump ball that defeated North Carolina in the 1971 ACC tournament championship game, seven footer Danny Traylor and Casey Manning were juniors.

A future Gamecock and NBA great, 6-4 Brian Winters, joined them as a sophomore and McGuire put a formidable lineup on the floor. Rick Mousa, Jimmy Powell and Ed Peterson came off the bench to help. Peterson was the designated bomber who broke up zone defenses with his long range shots.

The news media was curious as to how McGuire would approach his first season as an independent. Columnist Bob Quincy of the Charlotte *Observer* interviewed the Irishman and produced a column entitled "Moods of McGuire."

Quincy wrote that McGuire at times could "dissolve his enemies at 50 paces," but "when McGuire is the Happy Irishman, he has no peer in charm school. Today Frank is in love with the world."

Being out of the Atlantic Coast Conference, McGuire told Quincy, "is actually a break."

Quincy noted McGuire was "a man who can talk about a pleasant landing even when he bails out without a parachute."

"We're happy...the team and me," McGuire told Quincy. "We're trying to prove something. It could be a great year ahead."

The wire services had failed to list South Carolina in their preseason top five teams, but Quincy stated they were of top twenty quality.

"Probably saved us some losses," Quincy quoted McGuire. "Any time you're in the top ten they all gun for you. I like being rated. Don't get me wrong. But it can work in reverse."

With South Carolina out of the ACC, Quincy said they would be contenders, but "For what?"

For an NCAA berth, he answered his own question.

"We're like the Harlem Globetrotters," said McGuire. "We'll play anywhere there is a good box office."

McGuire added, "Sure I'll miss the ACC. "It was familiar and that sort of thing is helpful. At every school I knew the doorman, the janitors, the holdover students and the conversation: 'Drop Dead'!"

McGuire said he was thinking about a starting lineup of Rick Aydlett, Tom Riker, Danny Traylor, Kevin Joyce and Bobby Carver.

"That's not to say they will be there all season," he added. "When I was at St. John's, we learned we had to change the lineup when the kids hit Madison Square Garden. Those who do best in practice sometimes flop before 18,000 people. We call them 3 o'clock ball players."

McGuire said South Carolina was "going to make money on basketball this year; big money. Television alone with two national games will bring us almost $40,000. What did we get in the ACC? Maybe $5,000. We play Marquette here on a Sunday afternoon and fifty states will see it. Yes, a Sunday game and all sides approved — the fathers, the president, the janitor."

One of his concerns as an independent, McGuire said, was officiating.

"When you are in a conference you pretty much know how the game will be called. On a free lance schedule, the officials will call some strange ones. In preparing for that, I'm calling all sorts of infractions during practice. I don't want my players upset."

In a separate story, Quincy noted "Tom Owens, the smooth, defense minded center, is gone and so is the controversial John

Roche, the man who owned the basketball. Returning to the wars are some of America's finest basketball players.

"The Gamecocks have size: 7-foot Danny Traylor and 6-10 Tom Riker, plus corner smoothie Rick Aydlett, who is 6-7.

"The Gamecocks have back court: Kevin Joyce is a premier guard who will set the pace. Bob Carver is a top flight shooter and scrapper.

"The Gamecocks have bench: Ed Peterson, Brian Winters and Rick Mousa off the frosh are blue ribbon boys. Casey Manning and Jimmy Powell have experience."

Quincy said the South Carolina schedule "resembles a map for a cross country flight," adding, "If the Gamecocks don't miss all the planes they're scheduled to ride, they'll finish in good shape for somebody's tournament in March."

In Columbia's *The State*, assistant sports editor Bob Cole wrote:

"Echos of an Atlantic Coast Conference championship are almost hollow by now; names like John Roche and Tom Owens etched in the record book for posterity, are but a memory. A new era in University of South Carolina basketball hastens."

The first three games were on the road. South Carolina disposed of Auburn 84-63 and then flew to San Francisco to win the Cable Car Classic by defeating Santa Clara 77-66 and California 67-59, becoming the first non-west coast team to win that tournament.

Riker scored 26 points against Santa Clara but managed only 5 against California. Joyce had 19 and 14, and big Danny Traylor, who scored 9 in the first game, was superb in the championship contest, totaling 23 along with 10 rebounds.

After the Gamecocks defeated his team for the Cable Car title, California coach Jim Padgett declared "South Carolina has all the ingredients to go a long way this year." However, he tempered his praise by adding, "If they lack anything, it would be speed and quickness."

Finally opening their home schedule on Dec. 18, South Carolina survived a scare from Virginia Tech to prevail by a single point, 77-76, when Kevin Joyce came through with seven clutch free throws and a key rebound down the stretch to the delight of 12,516 Carolina Coliseum fans.

Junior Allen Bristow, who was averaging 30.7 points per game, almost led the Hokies to an upset. He scored 31 but fouled out with 23 seconds left and Charlie Lipscomb's 12 foot shot at the buzzer was off target. Joyce led South Carolina with 21, Traylor scored 19, Riker 17 and Aydlett 10. Traylor had 13 rebounds, Riker 11.

South Carolina went on to win its first seven games before los-

Tom Riker dunks against Marquette.—*Thomas A. Price II*

ing by one point, 77-76, to Villanova in the championship game of the Holiday Festival in Madison Square Garden. Another one point loss, 72-71, to Marquette would be South Carolina's only home court defeat of the season.

In the Marquette game sophomore Ed Peterson came off the bench when Marquette went into a zone defense to protect a lead. Peterson hit seven of eight shots from long range, but the Gamecock rally still fell one point shy.

South Carolina's Tom Riker and Marquette's Bob Lackey were ejected for fighting and Riker fractured a bone in his left hand in the scuffle that would hamper his play for several games. Riker sat out a game against Manhattan but Danny Traylor scored 37 points and the Gamecocks won in a breeze, 116-78.

South Carolina trailed St. Bonaventure 17-1 before Ed Peterson came off the bench to score on four consecutive shots to start a comeback and South Carolina eked out a 61-59 victory.

Three wins, a six point loss to Iowa in the Chicago Stadium, and a seven game winning streak occurred before Houston downed South Carolina 95-85, in Houston.

Midway through January *The State* printed a story announcing that Alex English from Columbia's Dreher High School had verbally committed to South Carolina and would sign with the Gamecocks in March. English would become South Carolina's all-time scoring leader four years later.

South Carolina finished regular season play with a six game winning streak, including a 109-83 rout of Notre Dame, to earn an at large bid to the NCAA tournament with a 22-4 record.

United Press International ranked the Gamecocks fourth in the nation going into the NCAA tournament and the Associated Press placed them sixth. South Carolina was paired against Temple University in a first round game scheduled for William and Mary's new arena in Williamsburg, Va. The winner would advance to the East Regional in Morgantown, W.Va.

Harry Litwack, the master of the zone defense, was in his 19th season at Temple and earned the bid as champion of the Middle Atlantic Conference. Temple's record was 23-7. The Owls had won six straight since losing to Villanova, a team that had administered one of South Carolina's four defeats.

Litwack and Frank McGuire had been friends and rivals for many years. Temple was making its 13th appearance in a post season tournament while South Carolina was making only its third, second in the NCAA. The Gamecocks were hoping to erase memories of their quick departure from the regional at Raleigh a year earlier when South Carolina lost to Pennsylvania and Fordham.

South Carolina and Temple had met five common opponents. Both had lost to Villanova, the Gamecocks by one point and Temple by fourteen. Temple had defeated California 61-57, Fordham 75-60, Manhattan 73-62, and Pittsburgh 89-74. South Carolina had downed California 67-59, Fordham 100-77, Manhattan 116-78, and Pittsburgh 69-59.

Tom Riker led South Carolina in scoring during the regular season with a 19.2 average. Kevin Joyce averaged 18.4, Danny Traylor 14.7, Rick Aydlett 10.3, Brian Winters 8.3, and Bob Carver 7.3. Traylor averaged 11.2 rebounds per game, Riker 10.4.

Ed Peterson, South Carolina's "zone buster" from off the bench, quit the squad after 19 games and his long range shooting would not be available to attack Temple's zone.

Clemson coach Tates Locke likened Kevin Joyce to superman after the Gamecock guard had sparked two victories over his Tigers, 62-58 at Clemson and 77-64 in the final regular season game at Carolina Coliseum.

"Kevin Joyce is Clark Kent," Locke declared. "He's got to be Clark Kent. Nobody can tell me any difference."

Locke said his Clemson team played its best against South Carolina, but "Every time we'd get something going, they'd have a super player make a super play."

Litwack said his Temple team wasn't as talented as some he had had in the past, but few had worked harder.

"I don't think this team has the overall talent of our 1956 or '58 teams," both of which finished third in the NCAA tournament, he told Bob Cole of *The State*. "But these kids are dedicated players."

Litwack feared his 6-9 sophomore, Joe Newman, would be overpowered by South Carolina's 6-10 Tom Riker and 7-0 Danny Traylor.

"The boys representing South Carolina were All-America high school boys," Litwack said. "Joe is a raw boned boy with limited high school experience. Matching him against Riker is like putting a man against a boy."

Somehow, Litwack said, Temple would have to find a way to offset South Carolina's height advantage. He felt mental attitude might help offset the Gamecock advantages.

"We're confident and in good health, and we've had a couple of good workouts," he said. "We are young. We start three sophomores, a junior and a senior while South Carolina has pretty much a veteran club."

He felt defense would be the key.

"The defense will be the answer in this game. It will be an all out game for everyone. They're a high scoring team and it will be up to our defense to hold them down. Of course, we will do our share of running, too, when the opportunity presents itself."

As the Gamecock coaching staff feared, Temple's famous zone defense gave South Carolina fits and the Owls grabbed the lead after three minutes of play and South Carolina tried to play catch up until Danny Traylor scored on an assist pass from Bob Carver with 2:51 remaining and Tom Riker scored with 2:01 to give South Carolina and four point lead, 51-47.

Temple has used its match up zone to build a ten point lead early in the game and had led 29-25 at halftime.

Litwack abandoned his zone press in the second half even though it had caused ten South Carolina first half turnovers.

"I've only got seven boys I play and they needed some rest," he explained afterward. "Also, my big men were in foul trouble."

At halftime, Frank McGuire told his team the first half was the poorest half they had played all year.

"I didn't tell them Temple was making them play that way," McGuire said in post game comments.

Carver and Joyce came up with key steals that were converted into baskets that enabled South Carolina to come back. When South Carolina got a four point lead, McGuire wanted to employ his own zone defense, but decided against it.

"We had wanted all night to go into a zone to see how they would react," he explained. "But we wanted a six point lead" before employing that strategy.

Ollie Johnson scored 2 quick goals for Temple to tie the score, 51-51, with 50 seconds remaining. Joyce missed a shot but Bob Carver tipped the ball out to him and McGuire called a time out with 37 seconds left to set up a final shot.

Joyce had missed five attempts from outside in the second half but McGuire went to his 6-3 junior for the game winner.

The Gamecocks worked the ball out front and with seven seconds remaining everyone on the bench stood up as a signal to start the set play. A pick was set at the top of the key, Joyce dribbled behind the screen and fired from about 24 feet. The ball swished through the nets as time ran out.

South Carolina had won its first NCAA tournament victory, 53-51, and would advance to the regional at Morgantown.

Riker, who made 9 of 14 field goal attempts, was the game's high scorer with 23 points. Joyce had 12, Danny Traylor 11, and Traylor led the rebounders with 10, although the shorter Temple team outrebounded South Carolina 39-30. Ollie Johnson was the only Temple player in double figures with 16 points.

In retrospect, McGuire said "We should have penetrated more in the first half. We've played against a lot of zones this year and should have done a better job of getting inside."

Sports editor Leslie Timms of the Spartanburg *Herald-Journal* commented Harry Litwack "may not have invented the zone defense, but from the way the Owls play it, he certainly improved it."

West Virginia University had a beautiful new coliseum to host the NCAA East Regional, but hotel accommodations in Morgantown were is short supply. The South Carolina team was housed at Mont Chateau, the lodge at a state park several miles up the mountain from Morgantown.

Frank McGuire commented, "I looked out my window and saw a deer. I'm from New York. I had never seen a deer before."

The South Carolina athletic ticket office had sold 2,500 tickets for the first round game in Williamsburg but sold only 800 for the regional in Morgantown as many fans canceled out when they couldn't get nearby hotel rooms.

South Carolina was paired against North Carolina, a rematch of the 1971 Atlantic Coast Conference tournament championship game, and Villanova would square off against cross town Philadelphia rival Pennsylvania on opening night in Morgantown.

North Carolina, whose 23-4 record was identical to South Carolina's, was ranked second in the nation. The Gamecocks were ranked sixth.

The media made much of the matchup, but McGuire said it was only a game, not a crusade."

It turned out to be not much of a game. Kevin Joyce scored 21 points, including 9 of 9 from the foul line, but the only other Gamecock in double figures was Tom Riker with 10. Five North Carolina players recorded double figures led by George Karl with 18. Dennis Wuycik had 16, Steve Previs 13, Robert McAdoo 11, and Bill Chamberlain 10 as the Tar Heels blistered South Carolina 92-69.

In a consolation game the next night, South Carolina avenged its Holiday Festival loss to Villanova, 90-78, to finish the 1971-72 season with a 24-5 record.

Tom Riker closed out his collegiate career with 36 points and 16 rebounds. Kevin Joyce scored 19 and was named to the all-tournament team. Traylor added 15 points. Joining Joyce on the all-tournament team were George Karl, Robert McAdoo and Dennis Wuycik, and Hank Siemiontkowski of Villanova.

Joyce would be selected for the 1972 U. S. Olympic team and would compete in the Munich Olympics before returning for his senior season at South Carolina. Riker was named a first team All-America by the National Association of Basketball Writers; The Associated Press; and the United Savings Helms Foundation. He was a second team choice by United Press International and *The Sporting News*.

XVIII

South Carolina

vs

Indiana

December 22, 1972---South Carolina 88, Indiana 85

at Columbia

Never one to shy away from controversy, Frank McGuire stirred up a big one in April of 1972 when it was revealed he had dropped Clemson from the University of South Carolina basketball schedule.

The move became known when Clemson announced its schedule April 6 and said the series had been canceled at the request of South Carolina. The Gamecocks and Tigers had met continuously for forty years. The series darted back to the 1912-13 series and there had been no breaks since 1932.

"It shocked us just like everybody else," Clemson athletics director Bill McLellan said in response to media questions. "I thought everything was set and ready to go."

South Carolina athletics director Paul Dietzel said scheduling was left up to each individual coach and it was Coach McGuire's decision to drop Clemson.

McGuire had complained about unruly behavior by students seated behind the South Carolina bench and lack of crowd control in Littlejohn Coliseum when the Gamecocks played there. McGuire was away on a recruiting trip when the cancellation was announced but assistant coach Donnie Walsh, in reply to media queries, said it was South Carolina's desire to "pursue a national schedule."

The idea, Walsh said, "is to bring in as many new opponents each year as possible. Obviously, we will still have some people on the schedule for two years in a row by virtue of a return contract."

Walsh added the cancellation didn't preclude South Carolina playing Clemson "at some future date."

The series would remain dormant for five years before being resumed in the 1977-78 season, but the break would create a media frenzy throughout the spring and summer months.

The NCAA adopted legislation making freshmen eligible for

varsity competition and first year player Alex English immediately claimed a spot in South Carolina's starting lineup. He would start 111 consecutive games and score a school record 1,972 points.

Another freshman, Mike Dunleavy, would also play in 111 games during his career, starting all but the first six. He and English would go on to become stars in the National Basketball Association and Dunleavy would coach the Los Angeles Lakers and the Milwaukee Bucks.

While the two freshmen bolstered pre-season 1972-73 prospects, junior Brian Winters came down with mononucleosis which would slow him in the early going.

Kevin Joyce was back from the U. S. Olympic experience and was elected team captain. Seven footer Danny Traylor was also back for his senior year.

"I don't know what kind of season we'll have," McGuire said. "We could be very good if the young players come through, or it could be a so-so year. One thing I do know, Joyce and Traylor are very good basketball players. And so is Winters."

Joyce scored 20 points and English made his collegiate debut with 12 but the season opened on a disappointing note as South Carolina lost a low scoring game to Tennessee, 55-45 at Knoxville. Victories over Nevada-Las Vegas, Michigan State and Georgia Southern followed but the Gamecocks lost to Providence in the Utah Classic at Salt Lake City before downing host Utah in the consolation game.

Utah coach Bill Foster seven years later would become McGuire's replacement at South Carolina after first moving to Duke University.

Coach Bobby Knight brought his Indiana Hoosiers to Carolina Coliseum to do battle with the Gamecocks on Dec. 22, 1973. Indiana was undefeated at 5-0, and ranked ninth nationally. South Carolina's record was 4-2, but the Gamecocks had won 13 in a row at home since a one point loss to Marquette the previous season.

Quinn Buckner, a 6-2 freshman two sports star from Phoenix, Ill., was averaging 11.6 points per game for Indiana. Buckner was a starting safety on the Indiana football squad and immediately jumped into the starting lineup when he joined the basketball team.

South Carolina countered with its own freshman super star. Alex English was averaging 13.5 points and 9.5 rebounds for the Gamecocks. Among the upperclassmen, Steve Downing led Indiana with 22.6 points and 13.8 rebounds per game.

Kevin Joyce was South Carolina's scoring leader with 17 points per game and had 27 assists. Brian Winters, still weakened from mononucleosis, was nevertheless averaging 11.5 points while Danny Traylor averaged 10.8 and nearly 10 rebounds per game.

An All-America player with the Gamecocks, Kevin Joyce was a member of the 1972 U. S. Olympic basketball team.—*USC Sports Information*

The first seven minutes were nip and tuck before Indiana established a hot hand from outside and ran off seven consecutive points to take a 16-10 lead. John Ritter, Jim Crews and Steve Downing worked the Gamecock zone over and Indiana led by as many as 12 points before South Carolina abandoned the zone and went man-to-man. The Gamecocks closed to 30-22, but could get no closer and trailed by 10 at halftime, 40-30.

Joyce scored 14 of South Carolina's final 16 first half points to keep the Gamecocks within striking distance.

When Indiana went up by 16 points, 54-38, with 16:07 remaining, it was time for Joyce to take charge. He began hitting long jump shots from the top of the key to stymie the Hoosiers' aggressive defense and South Carolina's full court man-to-man press began to take apart Indiana's deliberate offense.

The Gamecocks caught up quickly and with 5:41 to play when Alex English took a pass from Mike Dunleavy, scored and was fouled. He converted the free throw for a 78-77 South Carolina lead.

There were seven lead changes from that point with Joyce firing a 15 foot baseline jumper with 1:47 remaining to give South Carolina an 86-85 lead. Indiana missed on several last minute opportunities and Brian Winters dropped two free throws with 19 seconds left for the final margin, 88-85.

Steve Downing missed for Indiana with seven seconds left and a jump ball was called. Joyce, as he had done against North Carolina in the 1971 Atlantic Coast Conference tournament, controlled the tap and time ran out on Indiana.

At one point in the second half Joyce hit seven consecutive Jump shots and for the night he made 18 field goals in 32 attempts and scored 41 points, 26 in the second half. he also had eight rebounds.

Freshman Mike Dunleavy, starting his first game, made seven of nine field goal attempts and scored 16 points. Downing led Indiana with 28 and also had 14 rebounds as the Hoosiers outrebounded the Gamecocks 44-33. Ritter and Buckner scored 15 each for Indiana.

"What would we do without Kevin Joyce?" Frank McGuire asked as he walked into the media interview room after the game.

"Kevin is simply outstanding. Teams key on him all the time. He never goes anywhere on the floor without somebody, several people going with him. But when he gets hot, look out. He's virtually unstoppable. he's our home run. That was a fantastic performance."

McGuire said South Carolina had come back from further behind, "but never against a team that good. Indiana is very good — great bodies and strong—and Downing is the best big man we've seen in two years, maybe the best since I've been at Carolina."

Harry Morrow, writing in the Charlotte *Observer*, said:

"Fact No.1 about Kevin Joyce has always been that he is a complete basketball player. Fact No. 2, which embellishes the first, is that he plays hard every game.

"And that is why South Carolina won a sensational game Friday night."

Morrow noted that Joyce's previous career high was 33 points the previous season against Niagara when South Carolina wiped out a 17 point deficit to win.

Joyce, at 6-3, started the Indiana game at forward due to a knee injury that sidelined Rick Mousa, but switched to his more familiar guard position in the second half when he made 12 of 19 field goal attempts. He played the entire 40 minutes.

"I feel better with the ball," Joyce said of switching to the back court and ball handling duties. "I think I can control the game better. I know what's going to happen."

He said Indiana played great defense.

"They use their hands and bodies. I was just hot. I was just going to keep throwing it up."

Joyce said he was begging McGuire for a time out in the second half but "he wouldn't give it to us. He's such a great game coach."

Bob Cole, writing in *The State*, said "Joyce—and a full court, man-to-man press—became the catalyst for the Carolina comeback which left a partisan crowd of 12,063 drained at the finish."

Joyce, in his Olympic uniform, was featured on the cover of South Carolina's basketball media guide and James Beck of the Charleston *Evening Post* said "South Carolina's front cover man finally has put it all together."

Noting the weather outside Carolina Coliseum was miserably wet, Beck said Joyce "brought misery to Indiana's ninth ranked basketball team."

Luther Gaillard of the Spartanburg *Herald*, wrote that Bobby Knight figured the key to whipping South Carolina was to key on Olympian Kevin Joyce.

"The strategy was sound," Gaillard wrote, "but Joyce didn't take it too well."

Gaillard felt the real difference in the game was in the turnover department. Indiana committed 15 turnovers to 7 for victorious South Carolina.

Doug Nye, sports editor of the *Columbia Record*, wrote "Never had there been a comeback quite like this one in Carolina Coliseum. And never had there been a performance quite like the one put on by Kevin Joyce."

Nye said the Gamecocks, "to be sure, had put on some impressive rallies since they moved into the coliseum five years ago. And there had been some higher scoring individual outputs.

"But this was different."

Indiana, traveling in a university owned airplane, flew back to Bloomington in the wee hours. Coach Bobby Knight, frustrated by the loss in Columbia, reportedly walked over to the darkened terminal building upon landing and kicked in a glass door.

XIX

South Carolina

vs

St. Bonaventure

Feb. 10, 1973---South Carolina 75, St. Bonaventure 74

at Olean, New York

South Carolina's basketball team left Columbia on Christmas Day in 1972 for New York City where the next day they would meet Villanova in search of the Gamecocks' second Holiday Festival Championship in Madison Square Garden.

It would be more accurate to say a portion of the basketball team left Columbia on Christmas Day. The squad had disbanded for a brief holiday after the Dec. 22 upset win, 88-85, over ninth ranked Indiana in Carolina Coliseum. Since half the Gamecock squad was from the New York area, that group preceded the remainder of the team to the Big Apple to have Christmas dinner at home.

Freshman Alex English, a Columbia native, wasn't the least big awed by the massive Garden. He scored 23 points and pulled down 13 rebounds to lead South Carolina to an easy 80-64 win over Villanova in the Festival's first round. New Yorkers Kevin Joyce and Mike Dunleavy scored 16 and 14, respectively. Brian Winters, battling mononucleosis, added 9.

In the interview room after the game the New York media asked English if he were awed by Madison Square Garden.

"Carolina Coliseum is a nicer place to play," he replied. "It's much nicer than this."

English was asked why, as a black youth he chose to remain in the South rather than leave the area since he was a heavily recruited prospect.

"Columbia is home," he replied. "It's a nice place."

South Carolina's other black player, senior reserve guard Casey Manning, had made ten consecutive free throws until he missed one in the Villanova game.

"Shucks," said Casey. "I missed a free throw. My first."

Kevin Joyce made 10 of 11 free throws in the semi-final game and scored 16 points as South Carolina outlasted Manhattan 79-69.

English had eight field goals to also score 16, but scoring honors went to seven footer Danny Traylor who had 25. Mono weakened Brian Winters didn't score a field goal but was four of four from the foul line as the Gamecocks made 25 of 30 free throws.

Frank McGuire faced his alma mater, St. John's, in search of his second Holiday Festival championship, but a player who stayed home proved to be the Gamecocks downfall.

McGuire had recruited Bill Schaefer four years earlier but the 6-5 forward had stayed in the big city. The St. John's senior burned the Gamecocks for 31 points, making 13 of 23 field goal attempts, to lead the Redmen to an 86-79 win and the Festival title.

Joyce scored 24, English 23 and Traylor 10, but the South Carolina effort fell short. English had 18 rebounds, Traylor 12. Joyce, English, Traylor and Manning were each saddled with four personal fouls to hamper the South Carolina effort.

St. John's coach Frank Mulzoff commented after the game, "Those who stayed can beat those who went away." Mulzoff played under Frank McGuire at St. John's.

Schaefer, who had 40 points in St. John's tournament opening win over Grambling, scored 112 in the tournament and was a unanimous choice as the Most Valuable Player. Joyce and English joined Schaefer on the all-tournament team along with Charlie Mahoney of Manhattan and Henry Wilmore of Michigan.

Following the Holiday Festival, South Carolina defeated Lafayette and Fairfield, lost to Virginia Tech, beat Davidson, lost to Marquette, and reeled off wins over DePaul, Illinois, Marshall and Toledo to stand 14-5 going into a two game trip to New York to meet St. Bonaventure in Olean and Niagara in the Buffalo Memorial Auditorium.

Brian Winters seemed to have recovered from mononucleosis, but the Gamecocks had other health problems. Mike Dunleavy was slowed by a sprained instep and Kevin Joyce had shaken off nausea to stave off defeat at Toledo and spark a three point, 77-74 win.

St. Bonaventure had dropped a two point decision to Virginia Tech, a team led by Allen Bristow that had drubbed the Gamecocks 81-68 at Blacksburg, and McGuire noted St. Bonaventure had never before lost consecutive games on its home floor.

What transpired that cold winter night in Olean was a collegiate basketball classic that resulted in a one point victory for South Carolina. All-America Kevin Joyce was the high scorer for the winners with 24 points, but three less heralded players came through in the clutch in the dying moments.

Seven foot senior Danny Traylor rammed through eight points in the last four and a half minutes after being held to three in the first

Danny Traylor was South Carolina's first seven foot basketball player.—*USC Sports Information*

thirty five and a half. Freshmen Mike Dunleavy and Mark Greiner proved to be the heroes at the foul line.

Greiner, who had made only 5 of 17 free throws all season, calmly swished a pair to give South Carolina a 73-70 lead with 24 seconds to play. Traylor fouled out moments later and 6-9 St. Bonaventure center Glenn Price cut the margin to one point with 2 free throws as 24 seconds showed on the clock.

Dunleavy beat the Bonnies' frantic full court press and was fouled with nine seconds remaining. He sank both free throws and South Carolina cleared out to avoid fouling and a possible three point play. Price scored with one second left to take game high honors with 26 points, but South Carolina had a 75-74 victory.

Brian Winters followed Joyce's 24 points with 15. Dunleavy had 14, Traylor 11 and Alex English 8, but the 3 free throws by Mark Greiner, 2 in the last half minute, were the difference.

"Didn't I tell you it would be decided by one point," were Frank McGuire's first words in the post-game media interview room.

"We are very happy to have pulled this out, especially the way our two freshmen dumped in those four free throws in the closing seconds," he added.

St. Bonaventure player Jim Wallace summed it up this way, "They made the foul shots when they needed them. We didn't."

Bob Davies, writing in the Olean *Times Herald*, attributed St. Bonaventure's defeat to the loss of Bonnies star Bill Moore on personal fouls.

"The Bonnies lost that 75-74 decision to South Carolina with precisely 4:29 left in the spine-tingler at the University center," Davies wrote.

"That's when Bill Moore picked up his fifth foul.

"It didn't seem that important at the time.

"After all, Moore had scored only four points and St. Bona held a 68-63 lead and the Gamecocks' Mark Greiner, a freshman, missed the first half of a one-and-one.

"But, despite all that came thereafter, that's when the Bonnies lost the game that thrilled the Saturday afternoon turnout of 5,925 fans and the millions of Eastern television viewers.

"However, without Moore's muscular presence on the boards, the Bonnies were in trouble.

"It was the 6-4 sophomore who had kept Carolina's 7-foot, 240 pound Danny Traylor from dominating the boards.

"Witness what happened without Moore.

"Traylor took the missed Greiner free throw and was fouled by Glenn Price; and converted both ends of the two shot foul.

"After Price missed a one-and-one with 4:04 to go, South Carolina took the rebound and went on the attack. SC actually took four shots before Traylor tapped in the final missed shot and it was 68-67 with 3:30 left on the clock.

"Steve Hocker eased the situation for the Bonnies with a shot from the top of the key at 3:15 and a 70-67 lead.

"But, again it was Traylor, rebounding at 2:52 and 70-69.

"The Bonnies missed another chance to put the game out of reach when Hocker missed a one-and-one attempt with 1:19 to go. This time Brian Winters rebounded and on another missed Carolina shot, Traylor put in the rebound layup, his 10th rebound of the second half and the Gamecocks were on top 71-70.

"The Bonnies took time out to set up the attack.

"With 40 seconds to go, Hocker took a short jump shot, but missed and Winters rebounded. Greiner was fouled, but, this time the freshman, who made only five of 17 at the line prior to this, coolly dropped both through for a 73-70 lead with 24 seconds showing.

"Traylor fouled out with 17 seconds left and Price made it 73-72. Bona again had to foul, this time another freshman, Mike Dunleavy, and he too responded in the clutch, scoring both ends of the one-and-one with nine seconds to go..."

Writer Bob Cole of *The State* wrote, "South Carolina climaxed a strong comeback with some late clutch rebounding by Danny Traylor and crucial free throws to pull out a 75-74 victory..."

Cole noted Carolina trailed by as many as 11 points in the first half and the Bonnies carried a 36-32 lead into intermission, and later enlarged their advantage to 7 points before Joyce led a charge that cut the margin to 58-57 with 9:25 remaining.

"A rebound layup by freshman Mike Dunleavy propelled the Gamecocks to their first lead of the game since the opening minutes, 59-58, and set the stage for a frantic finish," Cole reported.

"The Bonnies forged a five point lead, 66-61, with 5:21 showing on the clock and again Carolina fought back. Brian Winters matched a pair of free throws by the Bonnies' Bill Moore before Traylor went to work.

"The Gamecock senior, limited to 11 points but who nailed 15 rebounds for the day's work, hit a pair of free throws at the 4:27 mark to cut the St. Bonaventure lead to three, 68-65. After Glenn Price missed the front end of a one-and-one with 4:04 showing, Traylor fought his way for a crucial rebound and layup to leave USC only one back, 68-67, with 3:34 remaining.

"Reserve Steve Hocker flipped in a jumper from the lane, but Traylor came back with another tip in to keep Carolina within one, 70-69, with 2:25 showing.

"Price was guilty of a charging violation, but Joyce missed on a short jumper with 2:18 left and the Bonnies again had possession with a one point edge.

"Hocker went to the line with a one-and-one opportunity with 1:19 showing and missed.

"Traylor became the man of the hour when he grabbed a missed Winters jumper and put it back in for a 71-70 USC edge with 0:59 left in the game.

"The Bonnies raced down the floor and Hocker attempted a jumper that missed. Winters rebounded and with 0:24 left, Freshman Mark Greiner—who had made only 5 of 17 free throws for the season prior to Saturday's game—calmly converted a pair from the line as USC forged a 73-70 lead.

"Traylor fouled Price seven seconds later—it was his fifth personal of the game—and the 6-9 junior converted both ends of a one-and-one to pull the Bonnies to within one, 73-72.

"St. Bonaventure then put on a full court press in a desperate attempt for the ball, but USC beat it and Dunleavy was fouled with 0:09 remaining..."

Moving over to Buffalo, McGuire—who infrequently scheduled sightseeing side trips—took the team on a bus trip to Niagara Falls. The drive shaft fell out of the bus and the team was stranded for more than an hour until a substitute bus arrived. The breakdown caused cancellation of practice the day before the Gamecocks took on Niagara

Despite the missed practice, South Carolina downed Niagara 84-74 with five players scoring in double figures. Traylor had 23, Joyce and Winters 15 each, and the two freshmen, English and Dunleavy, each contributed 14.

Operators of ski resorts in the Buffalo and Olean areas were complaining about lack of snow but South Carolina experienced "the blizzard of '73" while the Gamecock basketball team was in upstate New York. Fourteen inches of snow in the Columbia area delayed the basketball team's return home. Fortunately, there were five days between the Niagara game and a home game with Villanova.

The Gamecocks defeated Villanova, Stetson, Fordham and Duquesne, losing only at Notre Dame by four points, 73-69, to finish regular season play with a 20-6 record.

South Carolina accepted an at large bid to the NCAA tournament, their third consecutive trip to the playoffs and were scheduled to play Texas Tech in a first round game at Wichita, Kansas.

XX

South Carolina

vs

Texas Tech

March 10, 1973--South Carolina 78, Texas Tech 70
(NCAA Tournament First Round)

at Wichita, Kansas

Getting into the NCAA tournament in 1973 was a lot more difficult than in later years when the field was expanded to 64 teams and unlimited at large bids were available to conference also rans and independents alike.

Only twenty four teams were invited to the Big Dance, and fifteen of those were automatic bids that went to conference champions. Nine at large bids were left for independents such as South Carolina. A 17-5 record with four games remaining put the Gamecocks on the bubble and speculation listed them among twelve teams under consideration for the nine spots.

Actually, only two of the four remaining games—home contests with Villanova and Stetson—were supposed to come into play, as the selections were to be announced Feb. 28, and South Carolina was scheduled to play Fordham that night, at Notre Dame March 3, and at home against Duquesne March 7.

While the news media was having a field day speculating on South Carolina's chances for post season play, Frank McGuire took a couple of days off in mid-February to receive the Downtown Athletic Club's basketball "Sportsman of the Year" award in New York City. Receiving the football "Sportsman of the Year" award on the same program was New York Giants back Joe Morrison, who ten years later would become South Carolina's head football coach.

Sports Editor Leslie Timms of the Spartanburg *Herald-Journal* speculated that South Carolina stood a good chance of landing an NCAA bid if the Gamecocks defeated Villanova and Stetson. South Carolina did just that, routing Villanova 77-53 and Stetson 81-52, and edged Fordham 77-72 the day the bids were announced, to improve its record to 19-5.

Should they not get the invitation to the NCAA playoffs, a bid to the National Invitation Tournament in New York is certain," Timms wrote.

James Beck of the Charleston *News and Courier* speculated that South Carolina's hopes might hinge on an investigation of Southwestern Louisiana, another team under consideration with a 22-2 record.

"Actually, South Carolina's hopes may hinge on whether Southwestern Louisiana is allowed to participate in the NCAA playoffs after continued accusations that the Louisiana school is in violation of NCAA rules. If SW Louisiana is bypassed, that would cut the group to 11 for 9 berths," Beck wrote.

He quoted Davidson Athletics Director Tom Scott, chairman of the basketball tournament committee, as saying, "The NCAA may be just a little leery of Southwestern Louisiana. If there is any doubt about them, the NCAA may leave them out. We wouldn't want to take them in and then have to send them home and pick someone in their place."

Southwestern Louisiana, accused of committing 125 violations of NCAA rules, was suspended by the national organization, but the suspension was lifted by court order pending completion of the investigation.

The committee picked both South Carolina and Southwestern Louisiana and both wound up in the Midwest Regionals as the NCAA for the second time deviated from prior policy and moved teams out of their home region to make up the strongest field possible.

Although Tom Scott had said no team would be moved more than one region, South Carolina was jumped two geographic zones from the East to the Midwest and assigned a first round game against Southwest Conference champion Texas Tech in Wichita, Kansas.

South Carolina All-America guard Kevin Joyce could have cared less. He was just happy to be going to the Big Dance.

"Wichita, Kansas sure isn't New York City," said Joyce, a native of the Big Apple, "but I can certainly tell you I'm looking forward to going there. Where they placed us is incidental because we have to play good teams regardless."

Frank McGuire also wasn't concerned over being moved out of the East region.

"We'll play anywhere," McGuire said. We don't mind being in the Midwest Regionals."

Executive Sports Editor Herman Helms of *The State* expressed disbelief that the Gamecocks were shifted from the East and jumped over the Mideast to be placed in the Midwest, but he wrote the assignment "didn't lessen the thrill of the bid."

Alex English drives to the basket.—*USC Sports Information*

"But why the Midwest?" Helms asked. "It is not uncommon for teams to be switched from one region to the next closest region geographically for the playoffs. It has been done in the past when one region had a surplus of good teams as the East did this year.

"But never has a team been moved out of its region past the next closest region and dropped into a distant region as was the case with the Gamecocks..."

Helms sought an explanation from Manhattan Coach Jack Powers, a member of the East selection committee.

"We were obviously overloaded with good teams in the East," Powers explained. "There were four independent clubs in our region which we felt had the records that demanded their selections to the playoffs. But since there are only three berths for at-large teams it boiled down to a case of elimination and that was tough.

"Our committee considered Providence the strongest of the four clubs record-wise. Syracuse was second. We settled on those two, and then had to make the difficult decision of choosing between St. John's (18-5) and South Carolina (19-5).

"Both the Redmen and South Carolina are fine clubs and both have played tough schedules. After much deliberation we chose St. John's on the basis of its victory (86-79) over South Carolina in the finals of the Holiday Festival, a game in a prestigious tournament which attracted much attention.

"So our three choices in the East were made, but we didn't feel that South Carolina should be left out of the playoffs. Our committee strongly recommended that the Gamecocks be picked and assigned to another region."

Sports Editor Dan Foster of the Greenville *News* quoted national NCAA committee chairman Tom Scott as saying the committee had planned to finalize its selections on Feb. 28 before games that night were concluded, but due to the closeness of the teams in contention, the committee held off until that night's results were known.

"If South Carolina had not beaten Fordham they would have become an alternate," Scott told Foster.

South Carolina did beat Fordham, 77-72, and Virginia Tech, which defeated Virginia that night, became an alternate. Since all invited teams accepted, no alternate was needed and Virginia Tech was left out.

That's how South Carolina wound up in Wichita to meet Texas Tech in a Midwest Regional first round game. The Gamecocks finished regular season play by losing a four point game, 73-69 to NIT bound Notre Dame, and defeating Duquesne 90-79, to take a 20-6 record to Wichita. The Associated Press ranked the Gamecocks 19th.

Texas Tech assistant coach George Davidson scouted South Carolina against Notre Dame and, although the Gamecocks lost, he told Henry Freeman of the Greenville *News* and Luther Gaillard of the Spartanburg *Herald*, "I don't think our talent is on a par with South Carolina."

Davidson said the Red Raiders hadn't faced a player all year "of the caliber of Kevin Joyce, and I don't know if we have anyone who can play him."

He added 7-0 Danny Traylor "has three years of experience and three inches of height on our post man and I think they have the edge on us there, and Brian Winters is playing exceptionally well."

The National Association of Basketball Coaches named Joyce to its second All-America team the day Joyce played his final game in Carolina Coliseum. He scored 20 points in the 90-79 win over Duquesne but top honors for the night went to Brian Winters, who scored 22. Joyce would also be named an All-America by the United Savings Helms Foundation, as well as second team by the Associated Press and United Press International.

Texas Tech brought a 19-7 record to Wichita and Coach Gerald Myers said his team had no super stars.

"Our guys just play together," he said. "That's been our secret all year."

Southwestern Louisiana, under indictment for 125 alleged rules violations, and Houston, both with 23-3 records, were matched in the other game of the doubleheader in Wichita State's Levitt Arena. SWL, led by superstar 6-2 guard Dwight Lamar, averaging 29.7 points per game, and coached by Beryl Shipley, was ranked 12th by United Press International and 14th by the Associated Press. Houston featured the world's tallest guard in six foot nine inch Louis Dunbar.

It was the night they turned the lights out in Wichita. NBC-TV was on hand to televise the doubleheader with Curt Gowdy doing the play-by-play. Coliseum officials dimmed the house lights and a spotlight shone on the lady singing the national anthem.

Officials didn't take into consideration the building had mercury vapor lights that required five to seven minutes to recycle when turned back on. The opening tap of the South Carolina-Texas Tech game was a little late, much to the chagrin of NBC-TV.

South Carolina started slowly and struggled to a 30-30 halftime tie and the Gamecocks trailed several times in the second half before righting the ship to advance to the regional in Houston.

Two of the Gamecock veterans got the job done—Kevin Joyce scoring 21 points and Danny Traylor adding 16—but Coach Frank McGuire, who was opposed to the freshman eligibility rule, had to resort to first year players to claim a 78-70 victory over Texas Tech.

"South Carolina basketball coach Frank McGuire pulled off a successful gut play here Saturday to enable the Gamecocks to advance to the NCAA Midwest Regionals Thursday in Houston, Tex.," executive sports editor Jerry Sanders of the Charleston *News and Courier* reported.

"It didn't show—in terms of play—down the stretch, but McGuire had a lineup of one senior and four freshmen holding off Texas Tech to claim a 78-70 opening round victory in Henry Levitt arena."

Actually it was three freshmen—Alex English, Mike Dunleavy and Mark Greiner—most of the way, along with seniors Joyce and Traylor, and all but Greiner had been starters most of the season. Freshman Bob Mathias, 6-7, was in the game the final three minutes after Traylor fouled out.

The Charlotte Observer reported, "South Carolina, playing the final 11:23 with three freshmen on the floor along with All-America guard Kevin Joyce and senior Danny Traylor, slipped past Tech..."

Junior Brian Winters fouled out at the 11:23 mark and the *Observer* pointed out that Greiner, his replacement, was from Charlotte's South Mecklenburg High School.

Texas Tech led 52-48 when Winters fouled out but South Carolina forged a 53-52 advantage on a basket by Traylor who was playing with four fouls. South Carolina was up six when Traylor went to the bench.

"It was up to Joyce to provide the leadership," Jerry Sanders observed.

"Texas Tech had little alternative but to try to get the ball and Joyce was the primary ball handler. He made six free throws down the stretch and finished with 21 points.."

Under pressure from the Red Raider defense, South Carolina's freshmen "refused to play like individuals who were on a high school court just a year ago," Jerry Sanders wrote.

"Joyce was the cool leader. He controlled the game for the last five minutes, and that was it," Texas Tech coach Gerald Myers stated in his post-game comments.

Traylor matched his 16 points with 16 rebounds before fouling out and English also matched his point total by getting 15 rebounds.

Rick Bullock led Texas Tech with 19 points, 13 of them in the second half. Ron Richardson added 17 and Ed Wakefield 16.

In the second game, Dwight "Bo" Lamar scored 35 points as the Raging Cajuns of Southwestern Louisiana denied Houston a chance to play in the regional it hosted by blasting the Cougars 102-89.

"I can't recall when we've had to overcome so much to win," Coach McGuire said after the game. "I felt we were very sluggish at the beginning of the game. We seemed tighter than usual. I don't know if it was the pressure of being in the playoffs or the aftermath of a tough physical game against Duquesne.

"I wasn't happy with our start, but I enjoyed the finish."

South Carolina was paired against Memphis State and Southwestern Louisiana against Kansas State on the opening night of the Midwest Regional in Hofheinz Pavilion on the campus of the University of Houston.

South Carolina received a jolt when freshman star Alex English suffered a tear in his left eyeball during a practice the day before. Despite the injury, English scored 19 points against Memphis State. Joyce had 15, Winters 14, Dunleavy 12 and Traylor 10, but Coach Gene Bartow's Tigers outrebounded the Gamecocks 49-27 and overwhelmed South Carolina 90-76.

Brian Winters drives to the basket in Carolina Coliseum—*Manuel Gaetan*

Larry Kenon, described by the media as "a 6-9 powerful but graceful giant, scored 34 points and had 20 rebounds to lead the rout. Mike Dunleavy came out of the rough and tumble contest with a broken tooth and a facial laceration that required two stitches. Memphis State would go on to win the region and battle perennial champion UCLA in the NCAA title game.

Kansas State edged Southwestern Louisiana 66-63 in the other game, holding Dwight Lamar to 18 points, and South Carolina had one game remaining, a consolation contest against the Raging Cajuns.

Six Gamecocks scored in double figures and South Carolina took a five point decision, 90-85, to finish the 1972-73 season with a 22-7 record. English, despite his eye injury, led the scoring with 22 points. Traylor had 16, Casey Manning hit 6 of 12 field goal attempts off the bench and scored 13, Dunleavy with his broken tooth had 11, and Brian Winters contributed 10.

Lamar led Southeastern Louisiana with 22. A short time later the NCAA came down hard on the Raging Cajuns, imposing the first ever "death penalty," and SWL was kicked out of collegiate basketball for several years.

XXI

South Carolina

vs

Creighton

March 4, 1974--South Carolina 78, Creighton 69

at Omaha, Nebraska.

With a minute and five second to play and the home team in possession, trailing by nine points, a pint whiskey bottle sailed out of the stands and shattered on the court.

The official typewritten play-by-play noted: "1:05 Technical foul, debris thrown on court."

Alex English stepped to the foul line—after the shattered glass had been swept up—and converted a free throw to give the Gamecocks a 10 point lead, 77-67 and South Carolina had clinched a classic victory.

The final score was 78-69.

Creighton University Coach Eddie Sutton called it: "One of the greatest college games I have ever seen and the first four minutes of the second half have to be the most perfectly played four minutes by two teams that I've ever seen."

South Carolina opened the second half hitting seven of eight field goal attempts in the first four and a half minutes, but Creighton kept within reach by making five of five.

Sports writer Bob Cole of Columbia's *The State*, said, "The Bluejays played well enough to have won most games, but not quite well enough when the Gamecocks were near perfect."

South Carolina shot 57.6 per cent in the first half and 57.1 for the game, making 36 of 63 field goal attempts. Creighton shot 53.4 per cent for the game, making 31 of 58. There was only one missed free throw, Creighton making 7 of 7, with South Carolina making 6 of 7, including English's technical conversion near the end.

The typewritten play-by-play, however, showed Mark Greiner missing a free throw in the first half and Mike Dunleavy missing the second of two with twenty five seconds left in the game to make the final score 78-69. Therefore, the Gamecocks apparently missed two free throws although Dunleavy was credited with making one.

Brian Winters went from the Gamecocks to a distinguished NBA career and had his jersey number retired by the Milwaukee Bucks.
—USC Sports Information

Since there weren't many missed shots there weren't many rebounds, with each team claiming 22. The home town statisticians incredibly credited Creighton with 27 assists on the Bluejays' 31 field goals. South Carolina was credited with 11 assists on its 36 field goals.

South Carolina went into the final regular season game of the 1974 season ranked 10th in the Associated Press poll with a 21-4 record. The Gamecocks were coming off a 104-86 rout of Houston in the Gamecocks' final home game and had received an at large bid to the NCAA tournament.

Three future National Basketball Association stars led the Gamecocks through the season. Brian Winters averaged 20 points per game, Alex English 18.3 and Mike Dunleavy 16.0

Creighton was ranked 19th with a 21-5 record and had also been invited to the NCAA tournament. South Carolina was to travel to Philadelphia to meet in-state rival Furman, champion of the Southern Conference, in an East Regional first round game at the Palestra. Creighton was paired against Texas in a West Regional first round game.

In a second day story after the classic in Omaha, Bob Cole wrote, "On a night when seniors were honored with awards in a special pregame ceremony, with a record home crowd of over 10,000 wildly partisan fans prepared to give them a royal sendoff to the NCAA playoffs, Creighton shot a sizzling 53 per cent from the floor and lost.

"Creighton Coach Eddie Sutton found it hard to believe. South Carolina Coach Frank McGuire was ecstatic, but admittedly amazed."

In his post game analysis, Sutton opined, "We really weren't aggressive enough in the first half and we really got hurt on the boards early, but we surely didn't play a bad game. I'd think we'd win most games at home when we shoot 53 per cent."

Sutton added he didn't think there was a great deal of difference in talent between South Carolina and Creighton and "On other nights we might have beaten them, but not tonight. South Carolina is the best team we have played this year. It's hard to judge on just one game but I think they're better than Marquette."

Marquette was one of three common opponents, Creighton winning 75-69 at Milwaukee and South Carolina edging Marquette 70-68 in Columbia. Both teams also claimed regular season wins over Dayton and Duquesne.

"I was very impressed with South Carolina," Sutton declared. "If they play as well in the playoffs as they did tonight they will go a long way."

Bob Cole's game story in *The State* said "South Carolina blis-

Alex English scores a layup.—*Billy Deal*

tered Creighton with a sizzling 57.1 per cent shooting performance and rode Brian Winters' career high 29 points to a convincing 78-69 victory over the Bluejays."

Cole went on to say the win before an Omaha Civic Center record crowd of 10,216 boosted USC's record to 22-4 while Creighton dipped to 21-6.

"The Gamecocks, who climbed to 10th in the latest Associated Press rankings, pulled away in the final three and one half minutes of the first half to a 38-28 edge at intermission and then fought off a Creighton rally late in the game," Cole wrote.

"Carolina built what appeared to be a comfortable 70-57 bulge with only 4:30 remaining in the game when the 19th ranked Bluejays scored eight straight points in less than two minutes to pull dangerously close. But the Gamecocks, playing a slow, deliberate offense, finally reached the one-and-one situation and sophomore Alex English converted a pair of free throws at the 2:02 mark to cut short Creighton's charge."

Winters, a 6-5 senior from Far Rockaway, N.Y., was described by Cole as, "a thorn in the side of the Bluejays from start to finish."

Winters made 13 of 22 field goal attempts and all 3 of his free throw opportunities in compiling his career high 29 points. Freshman Nate Davis made 9 of 10 field goals in compiling 18 points. English had 14 points, including 3 of South Carolina's final 4 field goals.

Doug Brookins led Creighton with 23 points and Ralph Bobick and Gene Harmon had 16 each. Bobick, who made 8 of 11 field goal attempts, was credited with 12 assists.

"These kids have been tested all year and they have continually responded," Coach Frank McGuire said of the Gamecocks in his post-game comments.

"They responded again tonight. They proved something to me that I didn't think they could do—win 22 games. It's been a phenomenal season for us and we're going to savor it for a few more hours before beginning to think about Furman."

The South Carolina media wrote controversy into the matchup of the Gamecocks and Paladins in the NCAA first round, noting that McGuire had dropped Furman from its schedule after the 1970-71 season.

Furman head coach Joe Williams, who normally didn't scout opponents, showed up in Omaha and watched South Carolina's classic win over Creighton. The personal scouting trip, coupled with the perceived revenge factor, apparently paid off.

Furman used a late surge led by its All-America player, Clyde Mayes, to defeat South Carolina 75-67 and knock the Gamecocks out of the NCAA tournament. Mayes made 9 of 13 field goal attempts and was 3 for 3 from the foul line, scoring 21 points. He also had 16 rebounds,

Meanwhile, Creighton defeated Texas 77-61 in its first round game and then took UCLA to three overtimes before losing in the second round.

XXII

South Carolina

vs

Virginia Tech

January 8, 1975—South Carolina 81, Virginia Tech 77

at Blacksburg, Virginia

Coming off a 22-5 record in 1973-74, expectations were high for the South Carolina basketball Gamecocks entering the 1974-75 season.

Brian Winters had taken his twenty points per game scoring average to the National Basketball Association, but all of the freshmen and sophomores from the previous season's top ten team were back along with a six foot nine inch transfer named Tom Boswell.

"A host of returning veterans, a redshirt 'big man' and some talented newcomers make Carolina one of the teams to watch in 1974-75," Bob Cole wrote in a pre-season assessment in Columbia's morning newspaper, *The State*.

The lead paragraph on Cole's story read: "The man in the street hints it, pre-season polls suggest it, even Frank McGuire admits it: South Carolina's Gamecocks may be among the nation's elite this season."

Cole acknowledged that successful basketball teams had become a way of life for McGuire and the Gamecocks, "but this year's club might turn out to be one of the very best the Irishman has assembled since coming to USC in 1964."

Most of the pre-season polls placed South Carolina in the top ten, some of them in the top five, but Cole noted that was "nothing new for the Irishman," beginning his 25th season as a head coach and the 11th with the Gamecocks.

"We don't mind being ranked," McGuire said. "In fact, that's what we're playing for, to be among the best in the nation. It puts extra heat on you, but we'll take it any time we can get it. Now, all we have to do is go out and prove it."

The returnees were led by two junior co-captains, 6-8 Alex English and 6-2 Mike Dunleavy. Nate Davis, a 6-4 sophomore, was

Alex English established a career scoring record at South Carolina before becoming a star in the National Basketball Association.
—Billy Deal; Denver Nuggets

coming off a sensational freshman season. Boswell had sat out a year after transferring from South Carolina State and was expected to be the big center that South Carolina needed.

The team, however, was nearly devoid of seniors with 5-11 Jimmy Walsh, younger brother of assistant coach Donnie Walsh, the only fourth year player on the squad, and he had played sparingly for three years.

Jackie Gilloon, a long haired assist specialist from West New York, N.J., and Golie Augustus, a 6-6, blue collar worker from Columbia were two freshmen who would make an impact on the Gamecock program in years to come. Bob Mathias and Mark Greiner were a couple of journeyman juniors who knew how to play.

"English and Dunleavy are just outstanding players and are giving us great leadership," McGuire enthused in an interview with Cole. "In the past teams have double teamed us a lot but I don't think you'll see too much of that this year. We've got Boswell and a lot of depth along the front line."

The Gamecocks breezed through Bucknell 88-74 before more than 12,000 fans to open the season in Carolina Coliseum. Dunleavy scored 28 points and Boswell started his Gamecock career with 15 and 11 rebounds. Davis scored 11 and had 10 rebounds and English quietly contributed 11 points.

After being ineligible for a year due to transfer, Boswell was glad to have his first game as a Gamecock behind him.

"I don't think I did as well as I can do, but it will get better," he said in an interview with Ken Burger of *The Columbia Record*. "I will have to because our opponents will get better."

It took just one game for the opponents to get better. The Gamecocks traveled to Norman, Okla., to meet the Oklahoma Sooners of the Big Eight Conference and were upset, 90-84, in a high scoring contest. Two South Carolinians on the Oklahoma roster contributed to the defeat. John Gordon and Billy Graham, both of Charleston, scored 5 and 8 points, respectively, with Graham grabbing 9 rebounds.

South Carolina then won four in a row, including its own Carolina Classic tournament in which the Gamecocks downed eventual National Invitation Tournament champion Princeton and Louisiana State.

In the Ocean State Classic at Providence, R. I., South Carolina lost two of three, including a one point overtime, 78-77, decision to St. John's, followed by two wins for a 7-3 record after 10 games.

Cassell Coliseum on the Virginia Tech campus at Blacksburg, Va., was one of the toughest places in the nation for visiting teams. In 14 seasons, Virginia Tech had lost only 20 of 143 home games.

The lighting was unusual and the steep angle of the stands created the illusion of playing in a canyon. Many heavily favored teams had fallen there, including South Carolina which had been dumped two years earlier, 81-68, to a Gobbler team that went on to win the National Invitation Tournament, led by the play of Allen Bristow.

Coach Don DeVoe's Gobblers featured three players with South Carolina connections. Barry Isom was a junior college All -America at Anderson College and Larry Cooke was a native of Camden. Mark Cartwright had started his career at South Carolina before transferring to Virginia Tech.

South Carolina's three losses in its first ten games had dropped the Gamecocks from a pre-season ranking of fifth to sixteenth in the Associated Press poll.

Mike Dunleavy, scoring against Davidson, became a star player and head coach in the National Basketball Association.—*USC Sports Information*

Before a sellout crowd of 10,000, the Gamecocks and Gobblers fought on nearly even terms throughout the first half with Virginia Tech going to the locker room with a one point advantage, 48-47.

South Carolina built a ten point lead after intermission only to see it dissolve when freshman playmaker Jackie Gilloon threw away a couple of passes. One behind the back effort flew into the stands, enabling Virginia Tech to tie the score at 75-75, and sent Gilloon to the bench to face the wrath of Frank McGuire.

The veteran coach put his rookie guard back in the game in the dying moments and two Gilloon field goals, along with a couple of key Alex English rebounds, resulted in an 81-77 Gamecock victory.

The Game story in the Charleston *Evening Post*, said, "Jackie Gilloon, South Carolina's freshman passing magician, made a hur-

Jack Gilloon was a flamboyant playmaking guard for the Gamecocks, 1975-78.—*Manuel Gaetan*

ried transition from goat to hero against Virginia Tech here Wednesday night.

"Coach Frank McGuire pulled the razzle-dazzle New Jersey freshman from the final minutes of a tight game when a Gilloon behind-the-back pass went awry, allowing Virginia Tech a chance to ultimately tie the score at 75-75.

"After a brief scolding, McGuire dispatched Gilloon back into the contest, and he promptly flipped in two successive baskets that allowed the 16th ranked Gamecocks to escape with an 81-77 victory."

The Charleston newspaper quoted McGuire as saying of Gilloon, "I don't know whether to kiss him or scold him sometimes."

Virginia Tech Coach Don DeVoe credited Gilloon's play with being the game's deciding factor.

"Gilloon really hurt us, "DeVoe said. "We didn't play consistently."

Cartwright, the former Gamecock, put the finishing touches on Virginia Tech's comeback from ten points down with two jump shots that tied the score at 75-75. After the second long range Cartwright bomb, McGuire sent Gilloon back into the game and he drove the lane for two consecutive layups.

Virginia Tech cut the margin to 79-77, but Nate Davis sank two free throws with six seconds left for the final four point margin.

"South Carolina is a poised basketball team," DeVoe observed in his post-game comments. "They got themselves in a position to control the tempo. They were super at the free throw line. Overall,, they played it smarter, got it where they wanted it and kept it there."

Although outscored on field goals, 32-29, South Carolina obtained its winning margin at the foul line, sinking 23 of 28.

Gilloon finished with 20 points, but South Carolina's high scorer was Mike Dunleavy with 22. Alex English had 17, Nate Davis 12 and Boswell 10. No Gamecock had more than 6 rebounds as Virginia Tech controlled the boards, 34-29.

Russell Davis scored 25 points for Virginia Tech to lead all scorers while Cartwright scored 12. Cooke scored 10 but the other South Carolinian on the Virginia Tech roster, Isom, did not play.

McGuire said South Carolina won the game on "guts."

"The only thing we don't have is experience," he said. "We were up by 10 and we lost the lead. With Roche and those other fellows (referring to former Gamecock stars), they'd have made it 20. They'd never have let them get the ball back."

If Davis had missed the final two free throws to give Virginia Tech the basketball trailing by two points with six seconds remaining, McGuire said he would have pulled the Gamecocks out of their zone defense.

"We would have pressed them," he said. Perhaps fortunately for South Carolina, Davis made both free throws.

Asked about Gilloon driving for two layups after being jerked out of the game and scolded, McGuire said, "That took so much guts for a freshman just out of high school to do what he did."

The Irishman also wasn't surprised at the long range shooting by Cartwright.

"We knew he could shoot. That's why we recruited him," McGuire said.

Rudy Jones, writing in the Greenville *News*, said "South Carolina's Gamecocks took a big step toward maturing into a play-off contender...with a scrappy 81-77 win over Virginia Tech."

Jones noted the Gamecocks played much of the game without Tom Boswell who was on the bench with foul trouble.

"Freshman Jack Gilloon, who improves with every game, made two clutch baskets in the final 1:27 to pull the Gamecocks from a 75-75 tie into a four point lead and two Nate Davis free throws clinched the verdict," Jones wrote.

South Carolina shot a torrid 61.8 per cent from the floor in the first half, but still trailed by a point at intermission. For the game, the Gamecocks shot 50.9 per cent but were 82.1 per cent from the free throw line.

The win was the 460th of McGuire's collegiate coaching career, 193rd at South Carolina. He would win 90 more times before retiring.

After winning the thriller at Blacksburg, South Carolina won 10 of 15 games to finish the regular season with an 18-8 record. The Gamecocks were passed over by the NCAA but received a bid to the National Invitation Tournament in New York City's Madison Square Garden.

South Carolina defeated Connecticut, 71-61, in the first round but then lost to Princeton, 86-67, a team the Gamecocks had defeated, 65-48, in December. Princeton went on to win the NIT.

In a three way race for team scoring honors on the season, Boswell averaged 16.5 points per game. Dunleavy averaged 16.3 and English 16.0. Davis contributed 11.6 points per game and the freshman, Gilloon, averaged 6.9.

The final 1974-75 record was 19-9, the first time in seven years that South Carolina had failed to win more than twenty games.

XXIII

South Carolina

vs

Western Kentucky

February 23, 1980--South Carolina 73, Western Kentucky 65 (2 OT)

at Columbia

Some said the Irishman didn't want to end it. He wanted to play on forever.

It took two overtimes to complete Frank McGuire's final game as a collegiate head coach. The result was his 550th collegiate victory, and his 283rd as coach of the University of South Carolina Gamecocks.

The glory days of John Roche, Tom Owens, Tom Riker, Kevin Joyce, Brian Winters, Mike Dunleavy, Alex English and other Gamecock super stars had faded. South Carolina had struggled to manage winning seasons over the past four years, finishing 14-12 in 1977, 16-12 in 1978, and 15-12 in 1979.

McGuire announced his retirement effective at the end of the 1980 season, nudged out the door by an administration that felt it was time for a change. The skids were greased by a $100,000 per year settlement for four years.

The final year was another struggle with few wins over quality opponents. A 61-53 loss to Furman at Greenville in McGuire's final road game left South Carolina going into his final home game with a 15-11 record.

The previous home game, an 83-76 win over Boston University, had drawn only 2,816 fans in 12,401 capacity Carolina Coliseum. Interest in the Gamecock basketball program had waned. McGuire called himself "a lame duck coach."

Columnist Bob Quincy of The *Charlotte Observer*, a long time follower of the Irishman's career, interviewed McGuire for a farewell column written with three games left in the final season:

"Frank McGuire calls it a countdown," Quincy began. "Three, two, one—and his 30 years as a college basketball coach are over.

Frank McGuire, the Smiling Irishman.
—USC Sports Information

"Pensioned off after 16 years at South Carolina, McGuire hides his emotions about as well as an elephant covers footprints.

"'Three games and it's all over,' says McGuire, his strong chin jutting forward. 'I wish the days could come all at once. I'm not going any place. A lame duck coach...'

"Later, he compares his position to a man awaiting a noose, then mixes his metaphor by adding, 'When does the ax fall'?"

Quincy described McGuire, at age 65, as "ruggedly handsome, an artistic tinge of gray seeping into his always-in-place reddish blonde hair."

The columnist continued, McGuire "has no peer in style. He walks into the practice arena wearing black alligator shoes with special soft soles. His garnet nylon jacket has not a Frank McGuire nameplate on the left breast, but a Frank McGuire embossed *signature.*

"On court, assistants Danny Monk and Kevin Joyce direct the workout. McGuire always has coached from afar—observing, injecting an order by megaphone, occasionally halting drills to take charge."

Quincy quoted McGuire regarding his staff, "I worry. These are two fine coaches. What will happen to them? And my office staff?"

McGuire said his final team had worked hard to give him a winning season, "and we have accomplished that," but he conceded, we aren't quite good enough for the NIT or the NCAA."

The final season had been a parade of honors for Frank McGuire as he was showered with gifts and praise when his team played on the road.

"At Kentucky I got all this silver and then they kicked my brains out," he told Quincy. "Worst beating (126-81) ever for a team of mine."

Saturday, Feb. 23, 1980 was declared "Frank McGuire" day at the University of South Carolina. The arena area of Carolina Coliseum was designated "Frank McGuire Arena" and a portrait of the coach was hung in the building as part of the ceremony surrounding his final game.

A Frank McGuire Scholarship Fund, which W. F. Putnam, vice president for athletic affairs, called "representative of the scope of Coach McGuire's interest in the university" was established.

The State newspaper, in an unsigned story, called McGuire's final game a last hurrah:

"After 42 years of locker room pep talks, jousting with officials, last second shots that dropped—and a few that didn't, it's time for The Last Hurrah!

"Frank McGuire, whose reputation and accomplishments span the ascendancy of college basketball from the dilapidated, band box gyms of the Thirties and Forties to the cavernous shrines that abound today, makes his final appearance as a basketball coach tonight."

The opponent was Western Kentucky and the Hilltoppers brought a 19-6 record to Columbia. The matchup brought back memories of a previous meeting between the basketball teams representing the two schools. In that one, Dec. 30, 1971, the Gamecocks edged the Hilltoppers 86-84 to win the Holiday Festival in Madison Square Garden.

McGuire, who had coached the University of North Carolina to a 32-0 record and the NCAA championship in 1957, flew to Chapel Hill, N. C., to be feted at a North Carolina game on the afternoon of his final South Carolina game.

He reminded the Tar Heel crowd that it was he who selected Dean Smith as his successor.

"I just want to get credit for one thing up here," he told the North Carolina crowd. "I selected Dean Smith. The AD said 'no,' but I went to the chancellor and he said, 'Frank, if you think that much of Dean Smith, okay'!"

Coach Frank McGuire huddles with his team during a time out.—*Billy Deal*

With that parting shot, McGuire returned to Columbia to lead the Gamecocks one last time.

In pre-game ceremonies McGuire was inducted into the USC Athletic Hall of Fame. The ceremonies continued at halftime when Lt. Gov. Nancy Stevenson declared McGuire Coach Emeritus.

"I think she was a little reluctant to kiss me," McGuire said afterward. "But I kissed her anyway."

The coliseum wasn't quite full but the crowd of 10,853 was well above the season average.

Bob Cole, writing in *The State*, described the final game as "a barn burner, requiring two overtime periods before his senior dominated squad presented him with a hard earned 73-65 victory over

Western Kentucky. Not until the final seconds could they breathe easy."

In his post-game comments, McGuire said, "In the years I've been coaching, including that tough fifty seven season when we went 32-0, I can't remember hugging anybody coming off the floor. But I hugged that big bear, Cedrick Hordges, tonight."

Hordges, a 6-8 senior from Montgomery, Ala., scored 25 points and pulled down 11 rebounds to lead the marathon victory. Jim Strickland scored 15, Kenny Reynolds and Mike Doyle 14 each, and the fifth starter, Tom Wimbush, contributed 5 points. Five Gamecock subs saw action in the game but none of them scored, including junior Zam Fredrick who the following year would lead the NCAA in scoring under new coach Bill Foster.

"When it all came down to the last hurrah," Bob Cole wrote, "Frank McGuire's final 40 minutes as a head basketball coach weren't his final 40 minutes."

The score was tied at 54-54 after regulation and, incredibly, neither team scored in the final 5:35 of regulation or during the first overtime period. Both teams erupted in the second overtime with South Carolina outscoring the Hilltoppers 19-11, to win by eight points, 73-65.

South Carolina started the game on fire, hitting 7 of its first 8 shots, and built an 11 point lead. The Gamecocks then cooled off, making only 4 of the next 15 and saw their lead dwindle to 3 points at halftime, 31-28.

Western Kentucky took a three point, 54-51, lead but Hordges cut it to one with a field goal and Jim Strickland made a free throw to tie with 5:35 remaining. Both teams went into a cat-and-mouse spread offense stall, looking for an opening that wasn't there, and neither scored the remainder of regulation and through the first overtime; 10 minutes and 35 seconds without a point.

"But the Gamecocks went to work quickly in the second overtime, to the delight of the partisan crowd of 10,853," Bob Cole reported in his game story.

"Forsaking the waiting game when they controlled the period-opening tip, Carolina went on the attack and Hordges responded with a baseline jumper after just 13 seconds had expired.

"Western Kentucky turned it over and Hordges, who also collected 11 rebounds, did his thing again, slipping in a 12-footer that rattled around before finally falling to provide USC with a little breathing room.

"Craig McCormick's basket pulled Western Kentucky within two and Hordges opened the door when he missed a pair of free throws at the 3:29 mark. Jack Washington's jumper at the line tied it at 58 with 3:03 left, and the crowd implored the Gamecocks to come to life.

"They did. Tom Wimbush hit one free throw and missed the second, but Hordges controlled the rebound and quickly popped in a 12 foot turnaround that staked USC to a three point edge with 2:33 remaining."

Cedrick Hordges averaged more than 19 points per game during his Gamecock career.
—USC Sports Information

McCormick made a three point play but the Gamecocks made three from the foul line to remain three points ahead with 49 seconds remaining.

Then the Gamecocks began a parade to the free throw line as Western Kentucky fouled in desperation. South Carolina made 9 of 10 down the stretch and would have been 10 for 10 but for a lane violation.

Point guard Kenny Reynolds, one of seven seniors on McGuire's final squad, said the Gamecocks went out in style.

Hordges, who would go on to a career in the NBA, led the all senior starting lineup with an average of 19.9 points per game. Mike Doyle averaged 12.6, Jim Strickland 10.7, Kenny Reynolds 8.5, and Tom Wimbush 7.5.

In a post-game interview, Doyle, said, "I'm relieved. The pressure is off. It's great to win one like this."

Reynolds, who played 49 of the 50 minutes, said, "I'm real tired. What can you say after going two overtimes? It was an excellent game."

"We were nervous and we didn't keep our offense going," McGuire said of the long scoreless period. "In the second overtime I told them to go to the basket and I think that made the difference."

Asked is he would campaign for a bid to the National Invitation Tournament with a 16-11 record to prolong his career, McGuire said he could probably have an invitation for old times sake, but "I'd rather it come because of the worth of the team rather than on the reputation of the coach."

McGuire called the victory "as big as any one I've ever had. I wanted to go out with a win very badly."

He added, "I told the players that winning this game would be the best present they could give me. Its great to go out with 250 wins."

Reminded that he had won 550, not 250 games, the Irishman smiled, "I was only 300 off."

Sports Editor Leslie Timms of the Spartanburg *Herald-Journal* reflected on the McGuire career in a post-game column:

"The changing of the guard officially began taking place here Saturday night when Frank McGuire bade farewell to the University of South Carolina basketball program," Timms wrote. "He left in a more flamboyant style than he arrived.

"Between that first day that McGuire arrived at South Carolina in 1964 and Saturday night he has given the state some of its most unforgettable moments in sports He has been involved in controversy—more accurately has invited it. But he also built a basketball program at the university that attracted people as fans who had never set foot on a college campus nor viewed a college basketball game.

"Frank Selvy and Darrell Floyd at Furman and Grady Wallace from South Carolina had led the nation in scoring for four consecutive years back in the 1950s. Ironically, Wallace was leading the nation in scoring the year that McGuire's North Carolina team was winning the national championship. So, McGuire didn't invent basketball in South Carolina. But the combination of his charisma, the controversy and the fact that an entire state could watch these talented basketball players from New York play basketball by way of television made South Carolina basketball the hottest topic in the state.

"Young Baptist and Methodist kids who had seen All-American John Roche make the sign of the cross before he shot free throws, thought that was a necessary part of the shooting process. That was the impact his successful teams were to have. The Gamecocks became one of only four teams in ACC history to sweep through the conference regular season unbeaten when they did it in 1970. McGuire's 1957 North Carolina team had been the first to accomplish it."

Ten days after coaching his final game, McGuire was in Greensboro to watch the ACC tournament when he was interviewed again by Bob Quincy of The *Charlotte Observer.*

"I never realized how pleasant it would be, this retirement," Quincy quoted the Coach Emeritus.

"You play basketball and you have a routine. It's concentrate on the game until the pregame meal, which is always at a set time.

Then its wait on the bus to the arena. Then wait for another bus back to the motel, or to the airport.

"Coaching is regimentation. It's like being in the army or in the marines. I think I'm going to like taking it easy. I'm going to like letting other coaches catch the bus."

There would be one last hurrah after the last hurrah in Carolina Coliseum for Frank McGuire. On April 26, 1980, more than 50 players from his 16 seasons at South Carolina gathered in the Frank McGuire arena to pay tribute to the retired coach in what was billed as the "Game of Games."

They ranged in skills from All-America players such as John Roche, who sports writer Ernie Trubiano of *The State* described as "the dominating force of a dominating era" down to bench warmer Pat Clark who spent four seasons on the bench watching more talented athletes perform.

Clark recalled, "One game we were way ahead and the crowd began chanting 'put Pat Clark in!' and Coach McGuire turned around to the crowd and asked 'Pat who?'

"Its a period of my life that I wouldn't trade for anything."

Asked what his role was in the Gamecock successful years, Clark, who came from Scranton, Pa., and became a book salesman after graduation, answered, "I'm the guy who gave Roche his confidence by driving by me for layups in practice."

"We guys on the bench didn't have to worry too much about being in shape, so we enjoyed the road trips," Clark said. "Especially New York—there was lots to do there.

"I'm proud that I was one of Frank's boys."

XXIV

South Carolina

vs

The Citadel

Dec. 19, 1980--South Carolina 83, The Citadel 81 (3 OT)

at Columbia

From its first venture on a basketball court, Oct. 30, 1908 against Furman, through the 1994-95 season, the University of South Carolina was involved in 60 overtime games. Of these, the Gamecocks won 32 and lost 28.

Forty five required one overtime period to decide a winner, and fourteen went through two overtimes. Only one required three overtimes.

The longest game in South Carolina's basketball history occurred on Friday night, Dec. 19, 1980 in the opening round of the Palmetto Classic, a Christmas Holiday tournament involving four South Carolina teams in Carolina Coliseum.

Ordinarily, a game with The Citadel wouldn't rank among the most memorable in Gamecock history. South Carolina has dominated the series, winning 64 of 87 games played between a 24-15 Gamecock win at Columbia in 1914 and a 69-65 win at Charleston in 1990.

When the Bulldogs took on the Gamecocks in the Palmetto Classic in 1980, South Carolina had a twenty six game win streak against The Citadel. One had to go back to World War II when, on March 4, 1943, in the Southern Conference Tournament at Raleigh, The Citadel defeated South Carolina 37-23.

The 1980 matchup, however, shaped up as a challenge for the Gamecocks who, in the words of an advance story in *The State*, had "whipped only a couple of small college foes in six games," while The Citadel came into the Palmetto Classic undefeated with a 4-0 record under Coach Les Robinson.

Legendary coach Frank McGuire had retired the previous February and Bill Foster, his replacement, had gotten off to a rocky start. Foster, who led Duke to a final four and a final eight in the NCAA tournament the previous two seasons, had begun his coaching career at South Carolina with three consecutive losses on the road.

McGuire's final squad had graduated six seniors, including an all senior starting lineup and the 1980-81 Gamecocks were frequently referred to as the nation's youngest Division I team.

The Gamecocks began play in the Wendy's Classic at Bowling Green, Ky., by losing to host Western Kentucky, 73-69. That's the same Western Kentucky that McGuire had defeated in double overtime in Carolina Coliseum nine months earlier to close out his long and illustrious career.

Foster's team then lost the Wendy's tournament consolation game to Iona, 79-69, and traveled over the weekend to Huntington, W. Va., to take on Marshall on Monday night, a team that McGuire's Gamecocks had routed by 40 points in Columbia, 106-66, the previous season.

The Marshall players had vowed to defeat the Gamecocks by a wider margin than 40 points, and they didn't but they came close, winning 116-85 for a 31 point margin.

Those of us among the support staff got our first dose of the Bill Foster temper in the locker room after that shellacking. He picked up a forty gallon trash can and smashed it against the wall, strewing used paper towels and other litter throughout the room.

The Gamecocks defeated UNC Asheville in their home opener, lost to Clemson and beat Biscayne to limp into the Palmetto Classic with a 2-4 record.

A Christmas tournament involving South Carolina, The Citadel, Furman and South Carolina State, didn't create a lot of enthusiasm. *The State* was so disinterested it didn't offer a separate advance story on the event, including it in a roundup story covering weekend activity by all collegiate teams in the state.

The apathy contributed to the smallest crowd for a collegiate basketball game in the history of Carolina Coliseum. Only 1,112 souls could truthfully claim that they saw the longest basketball game in University of South Carolina history.

There were a couple of echoes from the past the day before South Carolina took on The Citadel and Furman battled South Carolina State to open the Palmetto Classic.

An Associated Press story out of Denver reported that Donnie Walsh had been fired as head coach of the Denver Nuggets, and another dispatch from New York City announced that Frank McGuire had been named "Director of Intercollegiate Athletics" at Madison Square Garden. Walsh for many years was McGuire's top assistant at South Carolina. The retired McGuire would serve part-time in setting up college doubleheaders for the Garden.

Walsh, incidentally, rebounded in the NBA to become president and general manager of the Indiana Pacers.

South Carolina opened the Palmetto Classic by bolting to a 15-2 lead and appeared on its way to blowing The Citadel all the way back to the Ashley River. Bob Spear, who covered the game for *The State*, said "a stampede appeared imminent."

However, The Citadel refused to fold and battled back from a 27-13 deficit with 7:28 remaining in the half, to tie the score, 31-31, at intermission. In a stretch of 11:18 from late in the first half and into the second, South Carolina scored only 6 points on 1 field goal and 4 free throws, while The Citadel was 7 for 7 from the floor to take an 8 point lead, 57-49.

South Carolina rallied to a five point lead, however, and appeared to have the game won, 63-58 with 1:10 remaining.

Terry Tucker's layup and a tip in by Gerald Toney of the Bulldogs cut South Carolina's lead to one point, 63-62. With thirty seconds remaining, Jimmy Foster made a free throw but missed the second, and Wade Moore banked in an 18 footer for The Citadel to send the game into overtime.

South Carolina controlled the tempo in the first extra period but couldn't pull away and Greer Huguley's five footer with 23 seconds left tied it at 70-70, sending the game into a second overtime.

Ed Cornwell twice scored tying baskets, the second tying it at 74-74, and Felipe de las Pozas, a 6-5 Brazilian, scored for The Citadel with 22 seconds showing on the clock, knotting the score at 81-81, and a third overtime began.

The score was still tied with eight seconds remaining in the third overtime when Zam Fredrick canned two free throws to put South Carolina up 83-81. Brad Jergenson prevented a fourth overtime period when he blocked The Citadel's last second desperation shot.

"After 147 minutes, 59 personal fouls, one technical foul, 50 turnovers and innumerable missed opportunities, South Carolina's Gamecocks struggled to an 83-81 decision over The Citadel in triple overtime Friday night," Bob Spear's game story in *The State* related.

His lead paragraph said it all but the reference to 147 minutes was a little puzzling. Regulation basketball games are 40 minutes of playing time long, so 3 overtimes added 15 for a total of 55 minutes. No matter, it was a marathon that ended in thrilling fashion. Perhaps Spear was referring to elapsed time of day. Two hours and twenty seven minutes seemed about right, but who—besides Bob Spear— looked at his watch?

Spear reported South Carolina "generally controlled the extra periods, but The Citadel would not yield and received tying baskets from first Wade Moore, then Greer Huguley, and finally Felipe de las

Pozas before Fredrick and Jergenson pulled the Gamecocks to their third win."

The writer noted that after de las Pozas "banked home a 12 footer with 0:22 left in the third overtime to forge an 81-81 deadlock, the Gamecocks went to Fredrick."

He drove the lane, was fouled by de las Pozas, and calmly sank two free throws for the winning margin.

Bob Cole's sidebar story in *The State*, said, "South Carolina's Gamecocks pronounced The Citadel dead about midway of the opening half, only the Bulldogs weren't buying it."

Bulldog Coach Les Robinson said his team "had some opportunities but we could never get the lead or have the ball for the last crack with the game tied. I knew their getting the last shot would catch up to us sooner or later."

"I think we relaxed a little," Fredrick said in a post-game interview. "The problem was, they kept fighting back. I never thought we had it won until the horn went off at the end of the last overtime."

Freshman center Jimmy Foster said "I thought it was over in the first half. I thought they'd lay down but they didn't. I should have known better because I played three years with Greer Huguley in high school. That's his kind of game, to never quit until its over."

Coach Foster said, "We played everywhere from brilliant to poor. At times it looked like the first day of practice."

Fredrick, who would surge to the NCAA scoring title with a 28.9 average for the season, scored 25 points in the triple overtime game. Jimmy Foster had 20 and 14 rebounds, forward Kevin Darmody contributed 14 and point guard Gerald Peacock was in double figures with 12. Jergenson, freshman forward Kenny Holmes and guard Kevin Dunleavy each scored 4 points.

South Carolina defeated Furman 62-53 in the championship game of the Palmetto Classic and went on to a 17-10 record for the 1980-81 season, but didn't receive a post-season bid.

XXV

South Carolina

vs

Florida State

December 31, 1980–South Carolina 80, Florida State 78

at Miami, Fla.

The University of South Carolina basketball team was scheduled to play Florida State University in Tallahassee on December 30, 1980.

The only problem was, Tallahassee would be a ghost town that day. All of the Seminole faithful would be in Miami where Coach Bobby Bowden's football team was scheduled to meet the Oklahoma Sooners in the Orange Bowl on New Year's night.

Most of South Carolina's fans would also be in Florida. Coach Jim Carlen's football Gamecocks, led by Heisman Trophy winner George Rogers, were scheduled to play the University of Pittsburgh in the Gator Bowl at Jacksonville on the night of December 29.

John Lanahan, a member of the Gator Bowl selection committee, suggested the game would be an attractive draw if moved to the Jacksonville Coliseum. South Carolina officials thought that would be a good idea and approached officials at Florida State.

The FSU hierarchy didn't want any part of moving a home game to an area where thousands of Gamecock fans had set up temporary residency and countered with a proposal to switch the game to Miami, to be played at 1:30 p. m., New Year's Eve, in the arena at Miami Dade South Community College.

South Carolina Coach Bill Foster said, "Okay. We'll do that if you'll give my team tickets to the Orange Bowl football game."

A deal was struck and the Gamecock team switched its travel plans from Tallahassee to the former Playboy Hotel on Miami Beach. A couple of us on the support staff covered the football game in the Gator Bowl and joined the basketball team the next day.

Foster, in his first season after succeeding Frank McGuire as South Carolina's head coach, had lost his first three games but then had rallied to win five of the next six to take a 5-4 record to

Miami. The Gamecock early season schedule, however, hadn't been a giant killer and Foster's most significant win was a 74-70 decision over Texas. The Gamecocks had battled through three overtimes to outlast The Citadel, 83-81, in the longest basketball game in South Carolina history.

Florida State, under former Furman Coach Joe Williams, had a 5-3 record with wins over Missouri and Georgia and a close loss to Auburn.

The State referred to South Carolina as, "The youthful and outsized Gamecocks," who had "parlayed hard play and scrappy defense into a 5-4 record with a four game winning streak. Foster had inherited a roster that had lost six seniors from McGuire's final team.

Florida State, on the other hand, *The State* reported, was "a veteran team with size and some big victories already this season."

What the Gamecocks did, writer Gene Able reported in his game story in *The State*, "was throw a wrecking bar into the middle of Florida State's Orange Bowl festivities."

South Carolina upset the Seminoles 80-78 before a crowd of 2,500 that half filled the junior college arena. Apparently the 20,000 or so other Seminole fans in town were too busy gearing up for the Orange Bowl showdown with Oklahoma.

The Gamecocks jumped out to a 14 point lead in the first half but, as Able reported, "almost started their New Year's Eve celebration too soon."

Everything "seemed to be percolating just right when suddenly everything went haywire," Able wrote.

"With 7:25 left, USC was sitting on a 71-60 spread and working on strategy designed around the certain shot."

The Gamecocks missed 2 shots, committed 4 turnovers, and those miscues led to 10 unanswered FSU points that cut the lead to 71-70. South Carolina's halftime lead had been 49-37.

"In spite of hostile surroundings and a loss of momentum they refused to fold," Able reported.

"Kevin Darmody boldly drove to the basket and raised the margin to three with 3:25 left. The 6-7 sophomore did it again a minute later, missed the shot but was fouled. He made one of two to make the score 74-72.

Freshman Kenny Holmes was guilty of a bad pass but hustled down court and recovered the loose ball. He fed Darmody who was fouled, and sank two free throws to make the score 76-72 with 49 seconds remaining.

Bobby Parks and Mickey Dillard hit long jump shots for Florida

State but Gerald Peacock made two free throws and Darmody scored a layup to offset the threat. Parks' field goal at the buzzer cut the final margin to two points, 80-78.

"This was a big win; a big win," Bill Foster enthused in post-game comments. "We played well in the first half; very intelligently; the most effective basketball we have played all season. Then, in the second half we became 'Hold on Nellie!' and that was a lot my fault. I wish we had attacked the basket more."

Senior guard Zam Fredrick, on his way to an NCAA scoring championship, led the South Carolina attack with 29 points. Freshman Kenny Holmes had 15, sophomore Kevin Darmody 14, and freshman Jimmy Foster contributed 10 points and 8 rebounds. South Carolina out rebounded the Seminoles 37-31.

"It was a good win over a fine team, and it came on the road," Fredrick told reporters after the game. "We got away from the things we were doing that put us ahead but we settled down in the end."

Coach Foster thought it was his young team's biggest victory and freshman Kenny Holmes pronounced it his best game in a South Carolina uniform. Fredrick added it was a nifty way to wind up 1980.

Dillard led Florida State with 28 points, 6-10 senior Elvis Rolle had 16, and Parks contributed 14 points to the Seminole cause.

The Gamecocks welcomed in the New Year on Miami Beach and attended the Orange Bowl football game New Year's night as guests of Florida State. Their seats were two rows from the top in the end zone, prompting Coach Bill Foster to quip, "We're two rows below the blimp."

The Florida State football team suffered the same fate at the hands of Oklahoma as the basketball Seminoles experienced against the Gamecocks. Leading 17-10 in the dying moments, the Seminoles saw the Sooners drive the length of the field, score a touchdown, make a two point conversion, and deal Florida State an 18-17 loss.

The following day, Jan. 2, the Gamecocks flew from Miami to Johnson City, Tenn., where on Jan. 3 they defeated East Tennessee State, 72-68, to end an exhausting road trip.

XXVI

South Carolina

vs

Marquette

February 17, 1981—South Carolina 91, Marquette 89

at Milwaukee, Wisconsin

Two of the great fringe benefits of playing basketball in Milwaukee against Marquette are staying at the Pfister Hotel and eating the great German food served at Carl Ratches' restaurant.

Coach Frank McGuire and his namesake and protégé, Marquette's Al McGuire, had established a thrilling home and home rivalry which began with a 63-61 South Carolina victory in the 1966 Milwaukee Classic.

Both McGuires had retired when South Carolina went north to Wisconsin to play Marquette on February 17, 1981. Hank Raymonds was the head coach at Marquette and Bill Foster had succeeded Frank McGuire at South Carolina. Marquette entered the game with a 15-4 record. South Carolina was 8-6.

Brad Jergenson, a 6-8 freshman forward from Manitowoc, Wis., had been the object of a spirited recruiting battle between Marquette and South Carolina. He spurned the scholarship from Marquette in his home state for the warmer climate of South Carolina.

Jergenson would be coming home to play against Marquette in his freshman season. Two bus loads of friends and neighbors made the trip from Manitowoc and were among the sellout crowd of 10,052 in the Milwaukee Arena.

Jergenson was so excited when he came off the bench for his first action that the first time he attempted a shot he threw the basketball completely over the backboard into the stands. He recovered his composure to contribute eight points to an upset Gamecock victory. While Jergenson made only 1 of 5 field goal attempts, he was 6 for 7 from the free throw line and also contributed 6 rebounds.

Two years later, when Marquette visited Columbia, Feb. 27, 1983, Jergenson was also instrumental in a two point South Carolina victory. He scored the tie breaking basket as time ran out in a 66-64 South Carolina win.

Like most of Marquette's games, it was a rough and tumble affair in Milwaukee.

The Warriors were whistled for 35 personal fouls to 25 for the Gamecocks. Four Marquette players—Oliver Lee, Dean Marquhardt, Michael Wilson and Artie Green—fouled out, while two Gamecocks, center Jimmy Foster and guard Kevin Dunleavy, were also disqualified on five personal fouls.

When the smoke cleared, South Carolina had a 91-89 victory in a thriller that went down to the wire. Although outscored on field goals, 33-30, South Carolina converted 31 of 45 free throws to outscore Marquette by 8 points from the foul line.

Freshman center Jimmy Foster led the first half surge, scoring 17 points as the Gamecocks took a 42-40 lead. In the second half, however, soon to be NCAA scoring champion Zam Fredrick took over. He had 10 points at halftime, scored 21 in the final 20 minutes, and finished with 31 for the night's work. Foster finished with 20 and freshman forward Kenny Holmes contributed 17.

Holmes had hit a school record eleven consecutive field goal attempts in South Carolina's previous game, a 90-62 win over Manhattan. He made his first try against Marquette to stretch the record to twelve before missing his second attempt.

Sports writer Bob Cole, who covered the game for *The State*, wrote: "The problem with Coach Bill Foster's first University of South Carolina basketball squad is, it can't follow a script.

"Billed as the youngest major college team in America and given virtually no chance of making big waves this season, the Gamecocks prompted a tidal wave here Saturday night, outlasting Marquette 91-89, in their finest hour under Foster's guidance."

Cole reported the Gamecocks built a nine point lead with "just over two minutes remaining and then had to withstand a furious Marquette charge—as well as their own inability to convert free throws down the stretch—before recording their ninth win in fifteen outings."

After missing four consecutive one and one opportunities to open the door for a Marquette rally, South Carolina finally salted the game away when Zam Fredrick hit a pair at the line—his 30th and 31st points of the game—with 12 seconds remaining.

"The Gamecocks' 88-79 lead with 2:03 showing had dwindled to a single point when Fredrick, who played superbly and finished with a career high 31 points, hit both ends of a one and one with 12 ticks remaining," Cole reported.

Marquette's Glenn Rivers' basket with 6 seconds left cut USC's

Zam Fredrick led the nation in scoring with a 28.9 average as a South Carolina senior in 1981.—*USC Sports Information*

lead to 90-89, but the Gamecocks beat the Warrior press and raced it up the floor before Gerald Peacock was fouled with no time remaining. Peacock made one of two free throws for the final spread of two points.

"We played about as well as we can play," Coach Bill Foster said in assessing the game. "The thing that kept us in it was our offense because we couldn't stop them from scoring."

Marquette Coach Hank Raymonds said, "We simply couldn't turn this team over tonight. Turnovers are our bread and butter (South Carolina had only 10 turnovers). Fredrick did a great job penetrating and getting good shots and we didn't go inside enough. We just didn't get the job done."

Fredrick reflected on the period when South Carolina couldn't make free throws.

"They were going in and popping out. There's not a lot you can do when you're missing free throws. When I hit the first of the one and one I was elated and when I hit the second one I knew we had them. I knew we could go home."

South Carolina finished the season with a 17-10 record, including victories in its final three games, over Florida State, Boston University and Georgia Southern the last by a 116-69 score.

The Gamecocks were left off the NCAA tournament invitation list but fully expected a bid to the National Invitation Tournament which never came. They missed out on post-season play.

XXVII

South Carolina

vs

Purdue

December 11, 1982--South Carolina 59, Purdue 53

at Columbia

The 1982-83 South Carolina basketball team had about three weeks of extra pre-season practice which probably helped the Gamecocks compile a 22-9 record, the first time in nine years that South Carolina topped the twenty win mark.

Coach Bill Foster took his team on a Far East tour, visiting The Philippines, Hong Kong, China, South Korea and Japan. The Gamecocks played two games in Manila, two in Beijing, two in Seoul and one in Tokyo during the 17 day summer trip that was sponsored in part by the U. S. State Department, the Chinese government, Nike and the University of South Carolina.

In Manila, South Carolina defeated a Philippine college team and Crispa, the champions of the Philippine professional league. In China, the Gamecocks won a one point decision over the Beijing city team and lost a close game to the Red Army team that featured "Mister Mu," a seven foot, five inch, 375 pound, 35 year old Mongolian center, who was aided by the Chinese officials who allowed him to camp 8 to 10 seconds in the 3 second lane on offense.

South Carolina defeated a team of South Korean college all-stars, but lost a close game to the Korean national team that displayed some of the best long range shooters the Gamecocks had ever seen.

In Tokyo, South Carolina easily defeated the Nippon College of Physical Education which showed the influence of its coach having attended Kentucky Coach Joe B. Hall's summer camp. The Japanese college team wore uniforms similar to Kentucky's, used the Kentucky warm up drills, and patterned its play in the Kentucky style.

The Japanese, however, fell far short of the Wildcats in physique and ability. Nippon's biggest player was six feet eight, but he weighed about 160 pounds.

The South Carolina basketball team visited the Great Wall of China during a summer trip to Asia in 1982.
—Photo by Randy Herald

The 17 day Far East tour produced a 5-2 exhibition game record and enabled the South Carolina team to visit the Great Wall of China, the Forbidden City, Summer Palace, Ming Tombs, Red Square and other cultural attractions of China, sight see in Manila, Seoul and Tokyo, and enjoy two days of shopping and sight seeing in Hong Kong.

It also afforded the Gamecocks an opportunity to get a head start on preparations for the 1982-83 season, which began in November with a routine, 86-68, win over Armstrong State. Junior forward Kenny Holmes of Savannah, Ga., who was developing a habit of recording hot shooting nights, made 9 of 10 field goal attempts to lead the scoring with 18 points against the small college team from his home town.

Holmes had set a school record as a freshman by making 11 of 11 field goal tries against Manhattan and as a sophomore, made 10 of 11 against Clemson. In the second game of the 1982-83 season, he was only 1 for 6, but the Gamecocks won 71-67 over Western Carolina to take a 2-0 record to the Fiesta Classic in Tempe, Ariz.

Against Utah, where Gamecock head coach Bill Foster was once the basketball coach, South Carolina had to go overtime before pulling out a 67-63 win over a team coached by former Foster assistant Jerry Pimm. Utah shot 64 per cent in the first half, but South Carolina managed to lead at intermission, 34-31.

The Utes led by 4 points, 59-55, with 27 seconds remaining in regulation after Pace Mannion sank two free throws. Mannion fouled Duane Kendall and the 6-10 sophomore from Las Vegas, Nev., sank two free throws to pull the Gamecocks to within 2 points with 20 seconds left.

Jimmy Foster committed his fifth foul to send Utah's Chris Winas to the line. He missed both free throws, Kendall rebounded and fed Gerald Peacock, who passed to Kenny Holmes who sent the game into overtime with a jump shot.

South Carolina outscored Utah 8-4 in overtime to improve the Gamecock record to 3-0. However, host Arizona State edged South Carolina, 84-79, for the tournament championship and South Carolina dropped an 80-75 road game to East Tennessee State to go into a Dec. 11 home game with unbeaten (5-0) and 15th ranked Purdue with a 3-2 record and a two game losing streak.

Jimmy Foster had been named to the Fiesta Classic all-tournament team but had suffered a hairline fracture in his left foot and was playing lame. Trainer Jim Price, however, said Foster could play.

"The x-rays show it's a hairline split rather than a break," Price reported. "It hurts him when he runs on it for any length of time but the doctor says there's no reason he can't play. It just depends how painful it gets for him."

The injury to Jimmy Foster brought on a prediction of disaster for the Gamecocks from *Columbia Record* sports writer Bob Gillespie.

"Tonight's game between the Gamecocks and the Boilermakers looked like an early Christmas present for USC basketball fans; a matchup between a nationally-ranked opponent and a once beaten (actually twice beaten) Gamecock squad," Gillespie wrote.

"And then Jimmy Foster put his foot in it.

"That's Foster's left foot, the one with the hairline stress fracture of the third metatarsal bone. Because of that injury, the regionally televised contest may be changed from 'Clash of the Titans' to a disaster flick."

The game almost produced a disaster, but not on the playing floor where South Carolina produced a stunning upset, but off the court where the Gamecocks almost lost a head coach.

Bill Foster began experiencing a tightness in his chest and chest pains during halftime, with South Carolina holding a one point lead, 29-28. By game's end, he was perspiring profusely and was obviously ill.

One of my post-game duties was to escort the coach to the media interview area for a press conference. When I entered the coaches locker room, I saw Coach Foster lying on the floor with Dr. Emmett Lunceford, the team orthopedist, bending over him.

"He's having a heart attack. An ambulance is on its way," Lunceford answered in reply to my query.

As Coach Foster was being wheeled out to the ambulance, I escorted assistant coach Steve Steinwedel to the interview area and explained to the media that "Coach Foster is not feeling well and is being transported to Baptist Hospital, and coach Steinwedel will conduct the press conference."

The media, naturally, wanted to know more immediately and I left the news conference in charge of a helper and dashed to the emergency room at Baptist hospital, only to be told a decision had been made to transfer the coach to Providence Hospital because of its cardiac care unit.

Eleven months earlier, I had gone through a similar experience. I spent several days in Baptist Hospital undergoing tests before being transferred to Providence where I underwent quadruple by-pass surgery to alleviate blocked arteries surrounding the heart. For the next few weeks I answered a lot of media questions comparing my experience with what Coach Bill Foster was going through.

The game was thrilling enough to give even the healthiest of fans a heart attack.

"The offensive impetus for the win, which ran USC's record to 4-2 while handing the Boilermakers their first loss in six games, came from a pair of back-to-back second half spurts, one by Brad Jergenson (perfect 5-of-5's from the field and at the line) and one by guard Harold Martin, USC's top scorers with 15 apiece," Bob Gillespie reported in the *Columbia Record*.

"Jergenson's streak kept the Gamecocks even with Purdue; Martin's put the Boilermakers away."

However, Gillespie concluded it was defense, "an area that especially let the Gamecocks down against East Tennessee," that made the difference.

"Purdue hit just 48 percent of its shots in the game, 42.3 percent in the second half, as the Gamecocks clamped down," Gillespie related. "USC, meanwhile, hit 52.8 percent, 60 percent in the second half."

Over a seven minute and twenty three second stretch in the second half, South Carolina's defense held Purdue to two points as South Carolina moved from a two point deficit, 41-39, to an eight point lead, 51-43, and the Gamecocks never trailed thereafter.

"The key was the job we would do tonight on (6-10 center Russell) Cross and (5-10 guard Steve) Reid," Steve Steinwedel told the news media while standing in for Coach Foster. "This was our best defensive job of the year."

Steinwedel said the Gamecocks did a good job defending Purdue's perimeter shooting in the first half but didn't do a good job against the inside play of Cross, who made all six of his field goal tries and had thirteen points at intermission.

Cross came into the game with a 17.5 scoring average and finished with 20 points, but had only 7 in the second half as the Gamecock defense limited him to 5 shots.

Reid, an outside shooter with a 15.6 average, managed only six points and got off only eight shots in the game.

Brad Jergenson credited the zone defense the Gamecocks called "three" with slowing the Boilermaker attack.

"The three defense really worked well the second half," Jergenson told reporters. He, centers Mike Brittain and Duane Kendall, and forward Jimmy Foster, collapsed inside on Cross.

"We kept one guy behind him, and the off man would sag back on him, the 6-8 Jergenson explained.

South Carolina trailed by as many as seven points, 16-9, before a Jergenson three point play began a comeback that gave the Gamecocks a 29-28 halftime lead. Jergenson scored the first eight South Carolina points of the second half to keep the game even.

Martin, who scored only three points in the first half, took command down the stretch. The 6-3 sophomore from Columbia tied the game, 41-41, with a jumper with 9:28 remaining on the clock.

In the next four minutes he canned a baseline drive, stole the ball and dunked it, hit an outside jumper on a feed from Kenny Holmes, and drained a 20 foot jumper from the corner.

"Everyone in Columbia knows I'm a streak shooter," Martin explained. "Once the rhythm starts going, I'm going to continue shooting."

The spurt by Martin lifted South Carolina to a 51-43 lead and over the final five minutes Martin, Jergenson and Peacock hit six free throws to hold Purdue at bay.

"That's what 'D' (defense) will do for you," Peacock said. "We didn't do that much on Cross but we figured if we could stop the other four we could win."

Cross scored 20 points but was the only Boilermaker in double figures. Peacock followed the 15 each by Jergenson and Martin with 10 points. Jimmy Foster played 30 minutes on his stress fractured foot but was limited to 6 points and 5 rebounds. South Carolina was out-rebounded by Purdue, 30-25.

Ernie Trubiano, writing in *The State*, called the South Carolina win "a major upset," pointing out Purdue was ranked 15th by one wire service and 20th by another.

Trubiano reported the game was "marred by an apparent heart attack suffered by the Gamecocks' head coach, Bill Foster." Trubiano added that Foster "has a history of hyper-ventilating after exciting games."

United Press International reported Foster "apparently suffered a mild heart attack near the end of Saturday's 59-53 upset victory against 15th ranked Purdue," and the Associated Press reported the coach was "taken from Carolina Coliseum by ambulance following the game after collapsing in the dressing room."

A later AP dispatch quoted me, as sports information director, as saying, "Indications are he's had a mild heart attack. His life does not appear to be in danger."

Mark Mayer, writing in the Florence *Morning News*, said "Sophomore guard Harold Martin scored 12 straight South Carolina points in the second half to ignite the Gamecocks to a 59-53 upset..." Mayer added, "Shortly after the victory, South Carolina basketball coach Bill Foster was taken by stretcher to Baptist Hospital with an undisclosed illness."

Luther Gaillard, in the Spartanburg *Herald-Journal*, reported, "South Carolina scored a major upset over 15th ranked Purdue Saturday night at Carolina Coliseum but the victory took on a somber tone when news arrived minutes after the 59-53 verdict was rendered that Head Coach Bill Foster had been taken to Baptist Hospital—with what was diagnosed as a "moderate heart attack."

Foster's condition, meanwhile, stabilized at Providence Hospital. Although Purdue had an early flight home the next morning, Coach Gene Keady and his wife, joined the Foster family and University of South Carolina officials in a vigil until about 4 a. m., at the hospital.

A catherization procedure dissolved the blood clot that caused the heart attack and minimized damage. Foster underwent quadruple by-pass surgery early Wednesday morning, four days after becoming ill. He wouldn't return to the Gamecock bench until the final game of the regular season.

Steinwedel, meanwhile, ran the team in the role of interim coach. After being upset by little Rider College, 63-56, in his first effort, Steinwedel led the Gamecocks through a six game winning streak and 10 wins in their next 11 games.

With a 20-8 record, South Carolina was left out of the NCAA tournament but received a bid to the National Invitation Tournament for the Gamecocks' first post-season play in five years.

With Bill Foster back on the bench directing his team, the Gamecocks defeated Old Dominion, 100-90, and Virginia Tech, 75-68, before losing in the NIT quarterfinals, 78-61, to Wake Forest to finish with a 22-9 record.

Bill Foster was a fierce competitor who survived a heart attack and by-pass surgery while coach of the Gamecocks.—*Manuel Gaetan*

The 1982-83 Gamecocks featured balanced scoring with only Jimmy Foster, at 17.3 points per game, averaging in double figures. However, point guard Gerald Peacock averaged 8.2 to rank fifth in scoring. In between were Kenny Holmes, 9.8; Brad Jergenson, 9.5; and Jimmy Hawthorne, 8.4.

Three weeks after ending the basketball season, South Carolina joined the Metro Conference, ending twelve years as an athletic independent following the Gamecocks' withdrawal from the Atlantic Coast Conference in 1971.

While remaining an independent in football, the Metro afforded South Carolina an opportunity to compete for conference championships and greatly simplified scheduling problems in basketball and other sports. After eight years in the Metro the Gamecocks would affiliate with the Southeastern Conference which would also bring football back into conference competition.

Steve Steinwedel's good work in filling in as interim head coach during Bill Foster's illness caught the eye of officials at the University of Delaware three years later and Steinwedel served nine years as head coach there, 1986-95.

The Blue Hens had some of their better years under his guidance, receiving their first two ever NCAA tournament bids in 1993 and 1994. However, he resigned under pressure after the 1994-95 season.

Bill Foster recovered from his by-pass surgery to coach three more seasons at South Carolina before he was dismissed by Athletics Director Bob Marcum and replaced by George Felton. Foster became head coach at Northwestern University in the Big Ten Conference for several years and then became associate commissioner of the Southwest Conference.

A testimonial dinner for him was held at Lancaster, Pa., in the summer of 1994 and was a reunion of many of his former players and assistant coaches. However, he missed it. Foster became ill on the eve of the banquet. Some months later he underwent by-pass surgery for the second time.

XXVIII

South Carolina

vs

Florida State

March 6, 1987--South Carolina 86, Florida State 85 (Metro Conference Tournament)

at Louisville, Ky.

The 1986-87 basketball season was a tough year for the University of South Carolina.

The Gamecocks under new coach George Felton managed a 15-14 record, an improvement over the 12-16 the previous season under departed coach Bill Foster. However, the program operated under a cloud. The National Collegiate Athletic association was investigating allegations of rules violations in previous years by the Foster staff.

Felton, a South Carolina graduate who warmed the bench and learned the game from Coach Frank McGuire, had been hired in hopes of restoring the glory of the McGuire years. In two seasons on the Gamecock team, 1974-75, Felton had played a total of twelve minutes in five games and hadn't scored a point.

As an assistant coach at four different institutions he had developed a reputation as a tireless worker and an outstanding recruiter. He returned to South Carolina from Georgia Tech where he served as associate head coach under another South Carolina alumnus, Bobby Cremins. Prior to his experience at Georgia Tech, Felton was an assistant at Appalachian State, North Carolina A & T and East Carolina.

Felton's first season produced a mixed bag. He lost three of his first four games then won four of the next five with a 79-62 decision over George Washington and a two overtime, 96-91, victory over Vanderbilt in the Sugar Bowl Classic at New Orleans the most significant. The Gamecocks lost the Sugar Bowl championship game to Villanova, 69-59.

At the end of the regular season, the record was 14-13, and South Carolina needed at least one win in the Metro Conference tournament at Louisville to finish above .500. In three previous Metro tournaments under Bill Foster South Carolina hadn't gotten past the first round. The Gamecocks hadn't really come close, losing in 1984 to Florida State, 75-69, and Louisville, 74-69, in 1985. In the 1986 tournament, Foster's last game as South Carolina's coach, the Gamecocks were blown out by Memphis State, 100-59.

The NCAA investigation occupied much of the media space and was a major distraction leading up to the tournament.

Newspapers quoted David Didion of the NCAA Enforcement Division that a letter containing "whatever, if any, sanction the (infractions) committee has decided on," would be mailed by Feb. 26, a week before the tournament. Didion, incidentally, would later leave the NCAA staff to become South Carolina's compliance officer.

The allegations contended that assistant coaches on Bill Foster's staff had sold players' complimentary tickets to boosters.

The Columbia Record reported "nearly 10 former players have claimed they sold their tickets to boosters for more than $500 and that a graduate assistant coach was the conduit for the sale.."

The newspaper continued, "Other players have claimed that assistant coach Ray Jones set up high paying summer jobs for them that required little or no work."

Bill Zack of the Spartanburg *Herald-Journal* identified the graduate assistant as Dave Blank. Blank had been a student manager under Foster at Duke and had transferred to South Carolina in the same capacity when Foster became the Gamecock coach. After graduation, he served as a graduate assistant on Foster's staff.

After the dismissal of Foster and his staff, Jones went to the basketball staff at the University of Minnesota and Blank was at Lock Haven State.

University of South Carolina officials conducted their own investigation and submitted results to the NCAA infractions committee at a meeting in San Diego. One of the committee members, University of Wisconsin law professor Frank Remington, told the Greenville *Piedmont* the NCAA's ruling was in the process of being finalized.

Amid these distractions, Felton and his staff attempted to prepare the team for the sudden death of the conference tournament. Point guard Michael Foster, the team's only senior, was recognized at the final home game, a 77-69 win over little Mars Hill College, and the Gamecocks upset Cincinnati on the road, 65-63, to finish the regular season with a two game winning streak and one victory above the break-even mark.

Meanwhile, delays in issuance of the NCAA ruling fueled speculation and kept the controversy going. The South Carolina Network, a radio news service, quoted an anonymous NCAA source that South

John Breckenridge blocks a last second shot by Florida State center Tony Karasek to preserve an 86-85 Gamecock victory in the 1987 Metro Conference tournament at Louisville.—*Metro Conference Photo*

Carolina would receive probation through the season nearly ended and the Gamecocks would be ineligible for post-season play, but the sanctions would not extend to the 1987-88 season.

Law professor Remington, the committee member who wrote the decision, called the South Carolina Network report, "inaccurate and erroneous."

David Didion said the report was "still in draft form and there could be more changes."

Finally, on March 3, just three days before South Carolina was scheduled to meet Florida State in the opening round of the Metro tournament, the ruling was announced. The Gamecocks received two years probation and were barred from post-season play in 1987, but there were no additional sanctions.

"We are pleased, if you can be pleased with this kind of activity, with the results, compared to what was within the purview of the committee to impose upon us," Dr. James B. Holderman, the university's president, said at a news conference announcing the action.

Holderman pointed out there were no restrictions on television, no reductions in scholarships, and "no findings of wrongdoing by any personnel presently at the University of South Carolina."

Felton issued a brief statement expressing relief that the investigation was over, placed his players off limits to the news media, and set about preparing for the tournament.

In third seed Florida State, sixth seeded South Carolina faced the Metro's hottest team. In sweeping its final three games to finish the regular season with an 18-9 record, the Seminoles under first year coach Pat Kennedy rolled up 330 points against Virginia Tech, Miami and Southern Mississippi.

The Seminoles out shot Southern Mississippi 117-102, after which Kennedy told news media with a straight face, "We won that one on defense."

In two regular season meetings, however, South Carolina had gained a split, winning at Tallahassee, 63-60, but losing to the Seminoles in Columbia, 80-72.

Terry Dozier had the game of his career against Florida State in the Metro tournament—38 points, 11 rebounds, 4 steals—but he had to share the spotlight with a seldom used Gamecock whose last second blocked shot preserved the one point, 86-85, victory.

During his four seasons on the South Carolina basketball team, 1986-89, John Breckenridge played in only 48 games and scored 66 points, an average of 1.375 points per game. Against Florida State in the 1987 Metro tournament the 6-10 sophomore played seven minutes and didn't score, but he became a media darling in the post game interview room because of one play.

Terry Dozier, the most talented of twin brothers on the South Carolina squad, scored the first 10 Gamecock points of the game and South Carolina managed a 4 point halftime lead, 44-40, making a 16-2 run at the end of the half to overtake the Seminoles who had forged ahead by 10 points, 38-28.

The second half featured 14 lead changes with South Carolina's 4 point advantage at 52-48, the biggest lead by either team.

"In the final minutes, the stars of both teams emerged to make the difference," Scott Peterson wrote in the *Greenville News.*

"Dozier, who scored more points Friday than in any other game of his career, was responsible for 8 of USC's final 12 points. Foster scored the rest, including one of his five 3-point shots. (Pee Wee) Barber, who was limited to 14 points on 4 of 14 shooting as a result of Foster's defense, scored 6 of FSU's final 10 points.

"Foster converted a four point play when he was fouled on a three point shot to give the Gamecocks the upper hand, 78-77, with 2:14 to play. Neither team led by more than one point thereafter as the advantage swung from side to side.

"Dozier and FSU's LaRae Davis and Jerome Fitchett were perfect in six attempts at the line and (Tony) Shaw canned a 12-footer from the baseline with 42-seconds left—his first field goal in 14 minutes to maintain the heart-pounding pace..."

Dozier's two free throws with 12 seconds left in the game put South Carolina ahead by one point but Florida State would have two chances to pull the game out.

The Seminoles attempted to set star guard Pee Wee Barber up for a drive to the basket but Michael Foster played him chest to chest and Barber's eight foot off balance shot missed. The rebound, however, fell into the hands of the Seminoles' 6-10, 240 pound Tony Karasek, who went up for a putback.

Breckenridge, in the game only because Darryl Martin had fouled out, made a clean block and swatted the ball to midcourt with one second left on the clock.

Ernie Trubiano, writing in *The State*, said the play "made a genius of USC coach George Felton, who inserted Breckenridge with 2:51 remaining and the Gamecocks trailing 75-72."

When asked about the strategy, Felton explained: "With Darryl already fouled out and with Perry Dozier with four fouls, I put John back in because I wanted to save Perry Dozier for the end, but I wound up keeping Breckenridge in there, and he did a good job."

Trubiano interjected, "That might qualify as the understatement of the year."

Felton called the play, "a big block; the biggest of the game; the biggest of his life; the biggest one on the team all year."

The block was Breckenridge's first of the season and second of his career.

He explained it this way: "When Barber's shot went up, I turned for the rebound, but he (Karasek) got a hip on me and got the rebound. When he went up, I was lucky to block it. I knew I hit all ball and no skin."

Staff writer George Borrer of the Louisville *Courier-Journal,* said, "All season, John Breckenridge has been hanging around for something like this.

"Last night, when it was time to come through for the University of South Carolina basketball team, he did."

Terry Dozier's 38 point effort set a new Metro Conference tournament scoring record, eclipsing by 1 the 37 scored 3 years earlier by Keith Lee of Memphis State.

Ernie Trubiano wrote that if individual awards were handed out in the wake of South Carolina's thrilling win over Florida State, the honors would go something like this: "Hero of heroes: Terry Dozier for his virtuoso, 38 point, 11 rebound, 4 steal performance which included the game's decisive points via free throws with 12 seconds left to help the Gamecocks to their first Metro Conference tournament game."

Dozier made 14 of 22 field goal attempts and 10 of 11 free throws.

"Best supporting role by a most unlikely candidate (and also best supporting role by a skinny 6-10 sub logging quality minutes for the first time in his college career: John Breckenridge for having the wherewithal to appear like an ashen ghost to reject a 'gimme' two-foot basket by 6-10 Tony Karasek at the 0:01 mark which would have given Florida State an 87-86 win.

"Best role-reversal role: Michael Foster, normally known for his scoring, made his biggest contribution on defense, harassing Seminole guard Pee Wee Barber into a forced, off-balance eight foot shot with four seconds left, setting up Karasek's rebound and Breckenridge's ensuing block. Foster also didn't forget how to score. The senior captain netted 15 points, including four of five home run balls. He turned his final three pointer into a four pointer when he converted the free throw after drawing a foul.

"Quietest 14 points: Tony Shaw who no one noticed until he calmly swished a 10-foot baseline jumper with 41 seconds left to give USC an 84-83 lead, setting up the heroics of Mssrs. Dozier, Breckenridge and Foster."

Trubiano's next-to-last award nominee was Florida State's LaRue

Davis for Best Player in a Losing Role. Davis scored 27 points, including six three point goals.

Finally, the Best Post-Season Dance Award went to George Felton, "whose victory prancing rivaled that of North Carolina State coach Jim Valvano when the Wolfpack won the NCAA championship a few years ago."

"I haven't learned which twin is which," Florida State coach Pat Kennedy said when asked about Terry Dozier's performance. "I don't know Perry from Terry, but I'd better learn because I've got to see him (Terry) for two more years."

Of his own performance, Terry Dozier said, "You can't ever predict having an outing like tonight, but I can't take all the credit because we had some guys play great defense at the end."

In pre-tournament voting by writers and broadcasters for the 10 player All-Metro Conference team, Terry Dozier came in 11th, and he said his omission motivated him to perform well not only for himself but for two teammates who he felt also deserved all-conference consideration.

"I felt like we had three of the top player (in the conference) on our team," Dozier said. "Darryl Martin was the leading rebounder, and Michael Foster is one of the top guards in the country, and I feel like I can compete with the best people in the conference."

Dozier followed his 38 point night by scoring 19 points in the second round against Memphis State, but the Gamecocks lost, 74-64, to end their season with a 15-14 record The game was considerably closer than the last time South Carolina had met the Tigers in the conference tournament. A year earlier, Memphis State had blown South Carolina away by 41 points, 100-59.

Sophomore Terry Dozier was named to the all-tournament team. He averaged 17.0 points per game for the season. Michael Foster averaged 16.2, Darryl Martin 13.6, Tony Shaw 9.8, and Terry Gould 5.8.

Martin, with a 9.3 average, led the Metro Conference in rebounding for the second consecutive season. A year later, as a senior, he missed out on a third rebounding crown, finishing a close second to Louisville's Pervis Ellison despite setting a Metro tournament record with 19 rebounds in a first round, 93-81 win over Virginia Tech.

XXIX

South Carolina

vs

North Carolina

Nov. 30, 1990--South Carolina 76, North Carolina 74
(Diet Pepsi Tournament of Champions)

at Charlotte, N. C.

South Carolina had some problems to solve as George Felton prepared the Gamecocks for the 1990-91 season, his fifth as head basketball coach.

Joe Rhett awaited medical clearance to resume playing after being fitted with a pacemaker. The 6-8 forward from Columbia had collapsed during a game the previous February as a result of an irregular heartbeat. A sophomore at the time, Rhett was South Carolina's second leading scorer with a 10.6 average and leading rebounder with 7.9 per game when his heart condition became known.

Guard Barry Manning didn't play in two pre-season exhibition games due to a ten day suspension meted out for violating some undisclosed university rules. Forwards Michael Glover and Stefan Eggers didn't play in the first exhibition—a 91-79 loss to High Five America—and 6-9, 250 pound Edmond Wilson, returning from a season as an academic non-qualifier, was carried off the floor with a mild knee sprain.

The loss to High Five America and a 67-64 loss to Sparta, a touring team from Czechoslovakia, didn't particularly concern Felton. High Five came in averaging 112 points in its previous 3 games which included wins over Pepperdine and Cal-Irvine.

"The first half we played pretty well," Felton said after the High Five game, "but fatigue caught up with us. We haven't put in our press attack offense, and it made a difference. We'll get that taken care of and I understand us being tired, because you can't play at that tempo and not substitute."

Rhett, cleared to play, came back with an outstanding performance, 25 points and 10 rebounds, but it couldn't offset a rash of

Gamecock turnovers, poor free throw shooting and the play of former Purdue All-America Troy Lewis for High Five.

"I wanted to come out and show everybody that even though I've got a heart condition, I can play," Rhett told reporters after hitting 9 of 12 field goal attempts for 20 points in the first half.

"Its uncomfortable when people keep asking how you're feeling and worrying about you, so I felt I had to prove myself tonight."

Earlier, Rhett had said he thought twice about playing again after Loyola-Marymount star Hank Gathers had died of a heart attack shortly after Rhett developed his health problem.

Gathers collapsed on the court March 4, 1990 during a West Coast Conference playoff game. His death resulted in a lawsuit against Loyola-Marymount. Concerns over legal responsibility and

Joe Rhett scored 1,142 points in 101 games for the Gamecocks before his promising career was cut short by a heart condition.—*USC Sports Information*

insurance coverage had held up clearance for Rhett to return to competition.

The Gamecocks headed north to Alaska to open regular season play with a full roster, the health, injury and disciplinary problems apparently behind them.

However, there were other distractions. The face of basketball and other sports in the Southeast were heading for dramatic changes.

The Metro Conference was disintegrating. South Carolina had opted, along with Arkansas from the Southwest Conference, to expand the Southeastern Conference to twelve members after the 1990-91 season. Florida State was switching to the Atlantic Coast Conference. Cincinnati and Memphis State were moving to the Great Midwest.

South Carolina won two of three games in the Great Alaska Shootout, defeating Nevada-Reno, 63-61, losing a close game to Virginia, 65-59, and defeating Alaska-Anchorage, 72-59. The Gamecocks landed three players—Barry Manning, Joe Rhett and guard Jo Jo English—on the all-tournament team. Rhett was the tournament's leading rebounder.

The 2-1 Gamecocks had five days in which to travel home from Alaska and prepare for their first meeting with North Carolina's Tar Heels in nearly nineteen years.

It was the Diet Pepsi Tournament of Champions in the new Charlotte Coliseum featuring South Carolina vs. North Carolina and Houston vs. Iowa State on opening night. South Carolina and North Carolina had had many classic battles in the old Charlotte Coliseum on Independence Boulevard, but this would be their first clash in the big new building.

The Gamecocks and Tar Heels had last met in the NCAA East Regional tournament at Morgantown, W. Va., March 16, 1972 when Dean Smith's Tar Heels drubbed Frank McGuire's Gamecocks, 92-69. A year earlier, March 13, 1971, South Carolina had upset the Tar Heels, 52-51, at Greensboro to win the Atlantic Coast Conference championship in the most thrilling finish in Gamecock history.

Not many pundits gave the Gamecocks much chance against the Tar Heels who had won their first two games of the 1990-91 season against lightweight opponents and were ranked fourth nationally. North Carolina held blowout wins over San Diego State, 99-63, and Jacksonville, 104-61. Oddsmakers established the line at 25 points with North Carolina the favorite. At game time the line was 17 points.

However, the matchup stirred memories.

"Perhaps the most memorable game in the series came in South Carolina's final game as a member of the Atlantic Coast Conference," sportswriter Jim Gilstrap recalled in the Anderson *Independent-Mail.*

"A last second layup by Tom Owens gave the Gamecocks a 52-51 victory over the Tar Heels in the finals of the 1971 ACC Tournament."

Bob Lang of the Charleston *Post &Courier*, wrote that "Frank McGuire gets excited when he talks about South Carolina's last Atlantic Coast Conference game. And he is excited about tonight's renewal of the South Carolina-North Carolina rivalry in the Tournament of Champions in Charlotte."

McGuire told Lang, "Chapel Hill had us beat," but 6-3 Kevin Joyce soared over 6-10 Lee Dedmon on a jump ball to control the tap to Owens for the winning basket.

"How Joyce got that jump ball I'll never know," McGuire said. "That was one of the greatest wins."

George Felton tried to remain calm as the battle neared.

"I'm trying to keep a level head on this thing, even though the hype and the media coverage has been great," Felton said. "I think it means a lot not only to USC basketball, but to basketball in the entire state. It's a high level game and any time you play a team like North Carolina I think it enhances your program."

Sportswriter Jim Gilstrap offered the observation, "It will help, of course, if the Gamecocks play well."

Felton said the keys to South Carolina's chances would be, "how we handle pressure and how we execute offensively. North Carolina is a very talented team. They have a much better bench than they had last year and they have good leadership in their starting five."

The Tar Heel statistical leaders were two forwards, sophomore George Lynch, averaging 18.5 points and 7.5 rebounds per game, and senior Rick Fox, 13.0 and 6.5.

"If our team comes out and plays well and gives us an opportunity to win the game, then I'll be happy," Felton declared.

Andy Friedlander, writing in the Spartanburg *Herald-Journal*, described North Carolina as "an entrenched national power," and observed South Carolina "is struggling to regain lost prosperity."

Joe Rhett, who was two years old the last time the Gamecocks played the Tar Heels, told sportswriters, "We're really excited about this. Even though we've had some tough games already this year and we couldn't overlook them, we've known from the beginning that we want to beat North Carolina."

Columnist Ron Green, Sr., in the *Charlotte Observer*, wrote that supporters of both schools should pay tribute to Frank McGuire, who had coached both the Tar Heels and the Gamecocks to some of their greatest heights.

"Frank McGuire will be there tonight, in one of the good seats, wearing an expensive suit, looking like a million bucks, with that smile on his Irish kisser," Green wrote.

"He's just a ceremonial figure now, something called honorary director for the Diet Pepsi Tournament of Champions at the Charlotte Coliseum. But when North Carolina and South Carolina take the floor against each other for the first time since 1972 they could bow toward McGuire in appreciation for what he has meant to their programs."

North Carolina Coach Dean Smith said he agreed to play South Carolina again because of Frank McGuire. Smith was hired by McGuire as an assistant at North Carolina and became the Tar Heels head coach when McGuire left Chapel Hill.

Coach George Felton upset North Carolina and Houston to win the 1990 Tournament of Champions.—*Manuel Gaetan*

"We're doing this for Frank McGuire," Smith said. "He asked me if I would schedule South Carolina when George Felton took over, and I said why not?"

Many of the 22,680 fans who saw a classic battle of the two Carolinas weren't in the stands when Houston polished off Iowa State, 87-72, in the tournament's first game to remain unbeaten at 3-0. Houston would rest and watch the Gamecock-Tar Heel matchup, meeting the winner the following night for the tournament championship.

The Cougars obviously thought they would be playing the Tar Heels, especially at halftime when North Carolina took a 12 point lead, 40-28, to the locker room. A blowout appeared in the making.

The Tar Heels led by 14, 40-26, on a breakaway by George Lynch with 44 seconds remaining, but Edmond Wilson followed a miss by South Carolina freshman Jamie Watson with 25 seconds left to cut the halftime deficit to a dozen.

South Carolina was guilty of 17 first half turnovers and Dean Smith observed afterward, "We could have had them down 20 or 25 points at halftime."

However, the worm turned in the second half. Ron Green, Jr., of the Charlotte *Observer*, wrote that North Carolina "fell victim to South Carolina's quickness and defensive pressure."

Green said the Tar Heels, "working young players into crucial situations along with veterans, made an uncharacteristic 28 turnovers against South Carolina, which seemed to gather confidence as the game progressed."

The game was tied when North Carolina's Hubert Davis hit a pair of free throws with 35 seconds remaining to put the Tar Heels up by two, 74-72. South Carolina's Chris Leso went inside for a tying layup with 23 seconds remaining and everyone in the coliseum, including Dean Smith, thought the Tar Heels would play for the last shot.

Ron Green, Jr., said in his game story, "The Tar Heels, despite Dean Smith's wishes, didn't wait to take the last shot."

Davis fired a jumper from the baseline with 16 seconds remaining and South Carolina popped out with the rebound and raced up court on a three-on-two break. Barry Manning fed Joe Rhett who passed to Michael Glover, back to Rhett, back to Glover for a layup with eight seconds showing on the clock.

"I guess Hubert thought we were behind by one," Smith said in post-game comments. "I was hollering four corners. I was sure we would do it."

Davis said he knew the score was tied but he took the shot because "I thought there was less time on the clock."

North Carolina still had two chances to pull out the victory. They took a time out with 5.8 seconds left but then lost the inbounds pass. Joe Rhett was fouled with 1.7 seconds remaining but missed both free throws, North Carolina getting the rebound but Clifford Rozier's hurried shot didn't come close.

Final score: South Carolina 76, North Carolina 74.

The Heels would be in the consolation game against Iowa State. South Carolina and unbeaten Houston would play for the championship trophy.

The first few paragraphs of the *Observer* lead story by Ron Green, Jr., read: "After 18 years, the magic was still there.

"South Carolina stunned fourth-ranked North Carolina 76-74 Friday night in the first round of the Diet Pepsi Tournament of Champions at the Charlotte Coliseum, rekindling the glory days of a college basketball rivalry that went away but never died.

"Except for a brief moment early in the game, South Carolina didn't lead the Tar Heels until Michael Glover laid the ball in with eight seconds left to cap its gutsy comeback.

"When it was all over, after the Tar Heels had failed to score on two possessions in the final seven seconds and the biggest victory of his five year coaching career was secure, Gamecocks coach George Felton bolted into the Coliseum stands and hugged former coach Frank McGuire."

Felton told writers in the post-game interviews, "I think this sends some type of message that South Carolina is inching its way back. This certainly is a big win for us. We beat one of the premier teams in the country. Once we got close, I think our team felt they could win."

Glover, the only senior on the South Carolina squad and an undersized forward at 6-5, basked in the post-game glory.

"One day when I'm old," he said, "I'll be able to sit back in my rocking chair and, you know, tell my grandchildren about this one. I'll always remember it."

Joe Rhett said he grew up in Columbia admiring the North Carolina basketball program.

"I always looked up to North Carolina when I was a kid," he said. "I always wanted to play against them. It was a very emotional game for us. We felt it (the rivalry) very much."

With the score tied, 74-74, Jim Gilstrap of the Anderson *Independent-Mail*, described the final 24 seconds:

"Even then North Carolina came down the floor and ended up with a pretty decent shot. But a short jumper by Hubert Davis bounced off the rim, and Leso pulled down the rebound and cleared the ball to Barry Manning.

"Manning then found Joe Rhett, running almost free toward the basket. Rhett passed to Glover on the right side, and Glover pushed the ball back to Rhett. The final pass was to Glover, who drove in for the game-winner."

In the media interview room, Glover said "I was confident the ball was going in. I got the ball to Joe and was just happy he gave it back to me. King Rice was there, and I was sort of worried about the charge, but I tried to be careful, and it just went in."

Glover went on to say the team had been hearing all week about how the Gamecocks were over matched against the Tar Heels.

"We were hearing all week how we were going to get beat," he said. "All over Columbia, they were saying, 'Y'all might as well just come on back to Columbia because y'all got no chance'."

But in a true rivalry game, writer Stan Olson pointed out, "There is always a chance, no matter what the bookmakers say. Even Glover, who just turned 21, knew that."

Glover said, "I knew we could win in the second half. It seemed like they were getting kind of fatigued."

"They badly outplayed us in the second half," was Dean Smith's assessment. "They were down 14 (actually 12) at the beginning of the second half and kept coming back, believing they could win, and they did. They held their poise and were just outstanding. They certainly improved their shooting over previous games we've seen."

The Gamecocks made 66.7 per cent of their second half field goal attempts and shot 51.7 per cent overall, making 31 of 60. The Tar Heels were almost as accurate, shooting 50.9 per cent but didn't take as many shots, making 27 of 53. North Carolina made 79.2 per cent of its free throws, 19 of 24, while the Gamecocks made only 55 per cent, 11 of 20. However, the Gamecocks made 6 straight in the final 10 minutes.

Each team had 30 rebounds and South Carolina's offense turned in 20 assists to only 12 for North Carolina. Both coaches made extensive use of the bench, Felton using 10 players and Smith 12.

Five Gamecocks scored in double figures, Manning and Rhett getting 15 points each. Jo Jo English, who fouled out with 4:36 left in the game, scored 13, had 9 assists and 4 steals. Freshman Jamie Watson and Glover each scored 10.

George Lynch led North Carolina with 16 points, Rick Fox had 15 and Hubert Davis 14.

Second half turnovers were one of the keys. South Carolina, with 17 turnovers in the first half, had only 7 in the second for 24, while North Carolina turned the basketball over 28 times.

Barry Manning explained the second half comeback in these words: "The guys kept telling me they were open under the basket, but it's kind of hard to pass the ball when you're being trapped by three North Carolina players. They just about wore me out. At half-time we talked about it and made an adjustment to have everyone come to the ball and pass to the opposite side of the pressure."

South Carolina first tied the score at 72-72, with 49 seconds remaining on a clutch three pointer by Manning over Rice.

"I knew I had to take the shot," he explained. "I was trying to look King Rice off me. He pulled away, and I just turned it loose."

One sidebar story on the game began, "Let's not wait another 18 years before we do this again," adding, "None of the fire that marked this natural rivalry that was last active in 1972 was gone when they tangled again at the Charlotte Coliseum..."

The story noted the Gamecocks beat the Tar Heels on what is

Michael Glover scored the winning basket in South Carolina's 76-74 upset of North Carolina in the 1990 Tournament of Champions.—*USC Sports Information*

the next best thing to a home court for North Carolina."Columbia is only 100 miles from Charlotte, as the Gamecock flies, whereas Chapel Hill is some 25 miles farther away.

"But when the residents of those two campuses brought their basketballers together Friday night at Charlotte Coliseum, the Gamecocks might as well have been playing in Idaho or New Mexico, some place where they were visiting strangers in the early going.

"It was North Carolina's house, no question. You knew it would be but not to this extent. Anybody could buy tickets.

"The Gamecocks were booed so roundly when they trotted out for action, you could hardly hear their fans whooping for them. But when the Tar Heels loped out, they might as well have been Elvis."

A column by sports editor Randy Beard in the Anderson *Independent-Mail* called the Gamecock victory, "a night of magic South Carolina basketball fans hadn't seen the likes of since Frank McGuire was coaching the Gamecocks during their glory years of the late 1960s and early '70s.

"And guess who was on hand to enjoy every second of what was a truly amazing flashback Friday night?

"You better believe those Irish eyes were smiling again."

Bob Gillespie, writing in *The State*, said the evening "was an artistic success even before the final outcome. The elements of nostalgia from a memorable era were in place.

"Venerable Frank McGuire, who led UNC to the 1957 national title and the University of South Carolina to its greatest days in basketball, basked in the glow of a rivalry reborn—in large part by his hand.

Seated at midcourt, midway between the two benches—but shaded toward the Gamecock side—the 76 year old Irishman was dapper in a crisp blue suit with red tie and matching pocket handkerchief."

David Newton, South Carolina beat writer for *The State*, said, "It took North Carolina and South Carolina 18 years to get back together for a basketball game.

"It took 40 minutes to restore the excitement of the series.

"In a battle reminiscent of Atlantic Coast Conference struggles of yesteryear, the Gamecocks stunned fourth ranked North Carolina 76-74 Friday night on Michael Glover's layup with eight seconds remaining in the first round of the Tournament of Champions."

Beat writer Stan Olson of the *Charlotte Observer* wrote of the young faces performing on the court:

"A bunch of youngsters who were in diapers the last time North Carolina and South Carolina played basketball got a taste of what used to be Friday night in the Charlotte Coliseum.

"This used to be a fierce rivalry with a touch of nasty about it almost two decades ago, back before the Gamecocks left the ACC and they quit playing each other. But Friday night, the rivalry rose again in gutsy South Carolina's stunning 76-74 victory over No. 4 North Carolina..."

In the end, Olson concluded, "It was the favored Tar Heels who crumbled in the second half, allowing South Carolina to wipe out what was once a 14 point lead.

"And when it was over, many South Carolina fans simply stood at their seats, yelling deliriously while the folks dressed in light blue glumly filed out."

XXX

South Carolina

vs

Houston

December 1, 1990--South Carolina 74, Houston 70 (OT) (Diet Pepsi Tournament of Champions, Championship)

at Charlotte, North Carolina

Would the Gamecocks be emotionally drained? Would there be anything left?

After the stirring come-from-behind last minute upset win, 76-74, over previously unbeaten and fourth ranked North Carolina, could South Carolina come back twenty four hours later, knock Houston from the unbeaten ranks, and win the Diet Pepsi Tournament of Champions?

As sportswriter Jim Gilstrap put it in the Anderson *Independent-Mail*, "The last second miracles continue."

This time, however, the Gamecocks took a different route.

In Friday night's game, South Carolina rallied from a 14 point deficit to take their first lead, 76-74, with seven seconds left in the upset of North Carolina.

In the championship game the Gamecocks lost a 13 point lead, jumping out front 17-4 in the early going, but rallied in overtime to defeat Houston, 74-70, and claim the Tournament of Champions trophy.

In the consolation game, North Carolina bounced back from its upset at the hands of South Carolina to build a 20 point halftime lead and coast to a 118-93 win over Iowa State.

Houston shot only 25 per cent, making 8 of 32 field goal attempts, in the first half but South Carolina could manage only a 6 point lead, 32-26, at intermission.

The Gamecocks expanded their lead to ten early in the second half but Houston hit some three pointers and the Cougar defense forced some turnovers and the game was tied with twelve minutes remaining. The lead flip-flopped from that point to the end.

Regulation ended with the score tied, 66-66. South Carolina had two chances to win the game in regulation but missed. Rhett's fourteen footer from in front of the basket bounced off the rim and Jeff Roulston's tip bounced away at the buzzer.

Houston forced the overtime when Roger Fernandez hit a long three pointer over Rhett with 16 seconds remaining.

Barry Manning's three pointer on South Carolina's first possession of the overtime gave South Carolina, a three point lead, 69-66. With South Carolina leading 70-68, Houston had three chances to tie but missed, was guilty of a three second violation and then Derrick Daniels missed two free throws with 57.2 seconds left.

That led to a tip follow by freshman Jamie Watson with 22 seconds left and a 72-68 South Carolina lead. Houston's 7-1 South American center, Alvaro Teheran, had his shot knocked away by Gamecock seven footer Jeff Roulston with 50 seconds remaining.

South Carolina led 72-70 when Darrell Mickens scored for Houston and was fouled by Jo Jo English with 6.2 seconds remaining. Mickens tried to miss the free throw on purpose and grab the rebound, but was called for a violation when he stepped over the line.

Michael Glover took the ball out and threw a length of court pass to English who dunked it with three seconds remaining to give the Gamecocks a 74-70 victory.

"Chants of 'USC, USC' rained down from the crowd while South Carolina basketball coach George Felton hugged Frank McGuire on the Charlotte Coliseum court late Saturday after the Gamecocks had won the Tournament of Champions with a 74-70 overtime victory against Houston," Ron Green, Jr., wrote in the Charlotte *Observer*.

"In two nights, South Carolina (4-1) put together a stunning tournament, beating two unbeaten teams to claim the championship. The Gamecocks, coming off their emotional 76-74 upset of North Carolina on Friday night, were pushed to the limit again by the Cougars.

"But in the end, the Gamecocks found a way to make the plays when they had to be made."

Houston coach Pat Foster, in post-game comments, said of South Carolina, "In critical points, they got the job done. They got the loose balls and hit some shots when they needed to. We didn't do that. All in all, it was a pretty flat mess from front to back."

Joe Rhett, who was voted the tournament's most valuable player, said the Gamecocks knew Houston was a good team and "We expected them to start hitting their shots," after the Cougars made only 8 of 32 in the first half.

"Coach Felton just stressed to us to keep our composure," Rhett added. "We went to Alaska to prove something, and we had one downfall. (Won two of three games in the Great Alaska Shootout). We came here saying we were on a mission, and this time we didn't

Jo Jo English scores on a slam dunk.
—USC Sports Information

have a downfall. I know a lot of people don't give us much credit, but we're showing that we deserve it."

Rhett, who had 15 points and 6 rebounds in the win over North Carolina, scored 21 and pulled down 12 rebounds in the tournament championship game to lock up the MVP trophy. Jeff Roulston had his best game, scoring 15, and two other Gamecocks scored in double figures, Jo Jo English with 11 and Barry Manning with 10.

Michael Glover, the hero with the winning basket against North Carolina, contributed 9 points against Houston. Freshman Jamie Watson scored only 6 points, but 2 of them were crucial.

"The highly-recruited freshman guard sank a follow shot with 22 seconds left in overtime to spark the University of South Carolina to a 74-70 victory over Houston in the championship game of the Diet Pepsi Tournament of Champions," David Newton reported in *The State.*

Teheran, who scored 32 points in Houston's opening night win over Iowa State, was held to 14 against the Gamecocks as Jeff Roulston played his best game defensively in addition to adding 15 points to the Gamecock offense. Byron Smith led Houston with 18, Roger Fernandez had 15 and Darrell Mickens 12.

Rhett and Manning of the Gamecocks were named to the all-tournament team along with Teheran and Smith of Houston, and George Lynch of North Carolina.

Jeff Roulston credited maturity with the two upset victories in the Diet Pepsi Tournament of Champions and in three other games that went down to the wire.

"The thing I'm most proud of is we haven't lost our composure in five close games. A lot of the same kind of games last year went the other way because we got rattled at the end. We're all more experienced. We all played a lot last year, when guys were hurt and we had adversity. This year, we're not getting rattled."

Roulston called his performance "definitely my best game offensively," but he added, "I had a better defensive game against Nevada," the week before in Alaska. This was probably the best total game I've played. We're a good basketball team and we've beaten some quality teams this year. We had a goal to prove we could play with those people."

South Carolina outrebounded the taller Cougars in both halves, winding up with 47 rebounds to Houston's 38. Rhett led with 12, Manning had 8 and Roulston 7. The Gamecocks had 22 assists to 15 for Houston.

South Carolina shot just under 50 per cent from the floor, making 29 of 59. Houston shot only 41.1 per cent, making 23 of 66. After an 8 for 32 first half, the Cougars were 15 for 34, 44.1 per cent, in the second half.

South Carolina defeated Temple, Charleston Southern, Furman, St. Joseph's of Pennsylvania and Brigham Young to stretch its winning streak to eight games and its record to 9-1. The Gamecocks rose to 12th in the Associated Press rankings before losing to Maryland, 78-69, in the finals of the ECAC Holiday Festival in Madison Square Garden.

The remainder of the season produced some significant wins, including two over Louisville, but the Gamecocks lost eight of their last ten games and after regular season play and an opening round loss to Florida State in the Metro Conference tournament, the record was 19-12 .

Hopes for an NCAA bid went down the drain but South Carolina received an invitation to the National Invitation Tournament.

The Gamecocks reached the twenty win level with a 69-63 home court victory over George Washington but played the second round of the NIT at Siena and lost a close decision, 63-58, to finish with a 20-13 record.

Jo Jo English led the team in scoring with a 15.0 average for the season. Barry Manning and Joe Rhett averaged 12.6 each. Jeff Roulston averaged 9.3 and Michael Glover 6.8 points per game.

Despite coaching South Carolina to its eighth twenty win season and only the second since the retirement of Frank McGuire, controversy swirled around Gamecock coach George Felton. Speculation abounded as to his job security.

The State reported March 26, in a story by David Newton, that a multi-year contract was being worked out, patterned after the contract accorded head football coach Sparky Woods.

"Woods' contract has provisions for graduation rates and drug testing," the story stated. "Felton's contract, which expires after next season, will be part of the postseason review by athletic director King Dixon."

Newton said Dixon would not comment on negotiations with Felton, but he indicated any agreement probably would be a new contract instead of a continuation of the old contract.

On April 30, Bobby Cremins was in Columbia to be inducted into the South Carolina Athletic Hall of Fame, and was besieged by newsmen for his views since Felton was a former assistant to Cremins at Georgia Tech and both had graduated from South Carolina.

"I couldn't have been more proud of George than when they won that tournament at Charlotte," Cremins told reporters. "When they beat North Carolina and Houston, I just felt this is great. I thought, wow! There they go. They're off and running.

"But, truthfully, George had a tough ending. And, he's got to bite the bullet, fight back, and come back strong next year. I'm biased towards George because I love him like a brother, and I'm his biggest fan. He's just had a tough ending, but he won twenty games and I think he's done a great job here. I really do."

Two weeks later, May 14, 1991, a story under Bob Cole's byline reported: "George Felton will be terminated as head basketball coach at the University of South Carolina, and the remaining year of his contract will be paid off, *The State* has learned.

"The reason for the termination was unclear, but sources said the decision was the recommendation of athletic director King Dixon. Felton had one year remaining on a five-year contract and was thought to have been negotiating a new three-year or four-year contract with the school.

"Felton said he had a planned meeting today with Dixon to discuss the future of the program but was unaware of any decision not to retain him as head coach."

Later that day, the official announcement was made by Dixon that Felton had been terminated "after an extensive and consuming" review of the basketball program that had been ongoing since January.

"It was a detailed review by our entire staff," Dixon told a packed news conference. "We have explored every item which you could conceivably look at concerning the totality of the program. It was not one isolated incident."

Dixon denied rumors that Felton had a drinking problem had any bearing on the dismissal.

"I'm going to tell you that I unquestionably contacted every name that I could possibly get who cited any rumor concerning Coach Felton and looked into them. I checked them out, each and every one. I can tell you now there was not one rumor I've heard that I could substantiate."

The news media had a field day with Felton's dismissal and the way it was handled.

Sports Editor Bob Spear of *The State* took Dixon to task in a column, saying Dixon in the news conference, "preached a self-serving forty five minute sermon and never answered the question on every tongue. "Why? "He danced around questions with the agility of a dervish."

Dan Foster, in the Greenville *News*, cited "complaints of his players during and after the past season, disappointments in his recruiting, dissatisfaction that he did not attend more meetings of the Gamecock Club, plus a widespread feeling in the athletic department that Felton was not a cooperative member."

Ken Burger in the Charleston *Post & Courier* noted that Felton "was not a favorite of the media that covered his team. He was moody and brusque, and uncooperative and a general pain in the butt."

In the end, Burger concluded, "George was fired because George was a real jerk."

In his five years as South Carolina's basketball coach, Felton compiled a 87-61 record. Several weeks before Felton was fired, his top assistant, Eddie Payne, landed the head job at East Carolina.

Felton would return to Georgia Tech as a part-time assistant, then become an assistant at St. John's, and four years later—when Eddie Payne was named head coach at Oregon State in the spring of 1995—Felton would become Payne's assistant there.

XXXI

South Carolina

vs

San Diego State

Dec. 21, 1991--South Carolina 71, San Diego State 69 (2 OT)
(Texaco Star Classic Championship)

at San Diego, California

There wasn't much to distinguish the tenure of Steve Newton as South Carolina's head basketball coach.

Newton was hired after an exhaustive search by a committee that spanned nearly two months with more than sixty names being bandied about in the news media which degenerated into a feeding frenzy of speculation.

Once, the committee was in executive session in the lettermen's lounge at Williams-Brice Stadium when associate athletics director Sterling Brown, a committee member, left the meeting to go to the rest room. When he opened the door he stepped on two reporters — Andy Friedlander of the Spartanburg *Herald-Journal* and David Newton of *The State*, who were crouched on their hands and knees at the door straining to try and hear what was being said inside the room.

There was talk among the reporters of having the skinny Friedlander attempt to crawl into an air conditioning duct to eavesdrop on the meeting. Some of the writers read an airline ticket coupon on the front seat of associate athletics director Art Baker's automobile parked at the stadium and reported that Baker had been to Rhode Island to interview then Providence coach Rick Barnes.

Finally, after a fifty-seven day search, Murray State University coach Steve Newton was hired as the replacement for George Felton.

The Gamecocks won only 20 games in two seasons under Newton, compiling an 11-17 mark in 1991-92 and 9-18 in 1992-93. Those were the Gamecocks' first two years as a new member of the Southeastern Conference and the SEC records for the two years were 3-13 and 5-11.

There was one tournament championship, however. The Gamecocks won the Texaco Star Classic in San Diego in December 1991, needing two overtimes to defeat the host school, 71-69, in the championship game.

San Diego State was no basketball Goliath, winning only six games that season. However, the circumstances under which I followed that game, made it a memorable moment for me.

I was no longer traveling with basketball, those duties being carried out by assistant sports information director Brian Binette. Nevertheless, I maintained a keen interest and kept close tabs on the team's activities.

My wife, Margaret, enjoyed shopping at the outlet stores at Santee and we drove there on Dec. 21, 1991, checked into a motel and did most of our Christmas buying. I took along a radio and, after dinner that night, tuned in the game from the west coast, which began about midnight South Carolina time.

South Carolina took a 4-1 record to San Diego, defeating four not too strong opponents and losing a one point decision, 61-60, to Oklahoma. In the opening game of the San Diego tournament, the Gamecocks downed George Washington, 69-58, to move to 5-1. Joe Rhett made 8 of 10 field goal attempts, scored 20 points, and recovered 12 rebounds to lead the win over the Colonials.

San Diego State defeated Florida A & M, 94-90, to advance to the championship game with South Carolina.

San Diego State held a three point halftime lead, 31-28, but Carolina outscored the Aztecs, 28-25, in the second 20 minutes and the game went into overtime as Margaret fell asleep and I paced the motel room floor to stay awake as the hour neared 2 a.m.

Each team managed seven points in the overtime and the score remained deadlocked at 63-63. Margaret snored and I walked outside into the cold, December air for a minute to fight off drowsiness before the second overtime began.

I may have been the only person awake in South Carolina listening to Bob Fulton's play-by-play broadcast as the hour approached 2:30 a. m., on the East coast.

Each team scored 6 points to make the score 69-69, with 19 seconds to play in the second overtime. I don't know if I could have made it through a third five minute extra period.

South Carolina took a time out and David Newton's story in *The State*, which was published a day late due to missed deadlines, said, "Coach Steve Newton drew a play to go inside to Rhett or outside to guard Jo Jo English, who finished with 23 points.

"Rhett, the first option, took a pass from Barry Manning. He then spun to his right and faded away for a soft jumper over Nelson Stewart that made a frustrating night on the boards bearable."

Newton quoted Rhett as saying after the game, "I almost shot on my way down. The guy was on my elbow and I started to fall away a little bit. I had a feeling it was going through, but I still had to watch it.

The shot gave South Carolina a two point victory, 71-69, and sewed up most valuable player honors for the 6-8 Rhett who was playing with a pacemaker to control an irregular heartbeat. He made 9 of 16 field goal attempts against San Diego State and scored 26 points. He had 49 points for the tournament, hitting on 17 of 26 from the field, and had 12 rebounds in each game.

Rhett and JoJo English of the Gamecocks were named to the all-tournament team along with Joe McNaull of San Diego State, Bill Brigham of GeorgeWashington and DeLeon Turner of Florida A&M.

Writer Jim Lindgren of the Los Angeles *Times*, wrote that San Diego State "took nationally recognized South Carolina, winner of all but one of its contests, into double overtime before bowing..."

Hank Wesch of the San Diego *Union* reported, "South Carolina forward Joe Rhett hit a 10-foot turnaround jumper with 10 seconds left in double overtime to provide the Gamecocks with a 71-69 victory over San Diego State..."

Before the 1991-92 season was over, Joe Rhett would suffer a recurrence of the heart problem that had resulted in installation of the pacemaker in his chest.

With 17:54 remaining in the second half, and South Carolina leading Mississippi State 26-24, on January 26, Rhett collapsed on the court. After paramedics and doctors worked over him, 6-10, 260 pound teammate Edmond Wilson picked Rhett up and gently carried him to a gurney which wheeled him to a waiting ambulance.

His promising basketball career was over. Rhett's 16.8 scoring average and 9.0 rebounds per game for the season were career highs. His rebounding average ranked second in the Southeastern Conference.

South Carolina led Mississippi State by seven points with a minute and thirty two seconds to play, but lost, 60-57. The Gamecocks would lose 16 of their final 20 games.

The Newton camp would suffer a number of other setbacks, not the least of which involved recruit Carlos Turner of Louisville, Ky. The teen-ager landed in a psychiatric hospital after allegedly attacking his girl friend with a knife and attempting to kill himself.

Turner never enrolled at South Carolina.

XXXII

South Carolina

vs

Kentucky

March 5, 1994--South Carolina 74, Kentucky 73

at Columbia

To have said the University of South Carolina basketball program was in shambles when Eddie Fogler was brought in before the 1993-94 season to right the ship would have been an understatement.

In two seasons under Steve Newton the Gamecocks had compiled a 20-35 record, 11-17 in 1992 and 9-18 in 1993. Admitted, along with Arkansas, to membership in the Southeastern Conference, South Carolina's SEC record was 3-13 in Newton's first year and 5-11 in 1993.

There were questions concerning the signing of several recruits, including one who allegedly slashed his girl friend with a knife, along with other problems that beset the program.

New Athletics Director Mike McGee recruited a former Gamecock hero, Bobby Cremins, to replace Newton and Cremins was introduced at a heavily attended news conference. Forty eight hours later, Cremins—who had captained the 1969 and 1970 South Carolina teams in the glory years under Coach Frank McGuire—changed his mind and returned to Georgia Tech where he had built a dynasty of success.

McGee then turned to Eddie Fogler, the consensus national coach of the year who had led Vanderbilt to the regular season Southeastern Conference championship in 1993 and into the NCAA tournament's Sweet Sixteen, compiling a final record of 28-6. His four year record at Vanderbilt was 81-48, and in three seasons at Wichita State 61-32.

Fogler, who had played against the Gamecock glory teams for Coach Dean Smith at North Carolina, had never experienced a losing season in twenty five years as a collegiate player, assistant coach and head coach.

As a 3 year letterman at North Carolina, 1968-70, Fogler had

Coach Eddie Fogler defeated Kentucky in his first season at South Carolina.
—USC Sports Information

experienced 2 NCAA Final Four appearances and 1 National Invitation Tournament. In 15 seasons as an assistant under Smith at North Carolina, he had gone to 13 NCAA tournaments and 2 NITs, and had reached the final four 4 times, including a national championship in 1982.

Fogler became head coach at Wichita State before the 1986-87 season, and in 3 seasons there he went to 2 NCAA tournaments and 1 NIT. Moving to Vanderbilt before the 1989-90 season, he experienced 2 NCAA tournaments and 2 NITs in 4 seasons there.

Twenty five years, twenty five post season appearances, makes March madness a way of life. But, the cupboard was almost bare in the Gamecock Roost and Fogler faced the task of rebuilding from the ground up.

Refusing to attempt short cuts, Fogler insisted on starting on page one.

"It certainly was a rebuilding situation when we got here," the USC media guide quoted him before his second season.

"There are two ways to build something. You can build it the right way and have it last for a long time on a consistent basis, or you can try to build it quickly and in the meantime make mistakes along the way and then maybe it collapses because of taking the risks involved.

"We have chosen to build this program the proper way so that South Carolina is a long-standing consistent winner."

There are many pitfalls along the way to building a winner and Fogler's first team ran into just about all of them.

He had two veteran 6-7 seniors in Jamie Watson and Emmett Hall and a hard working 6-1 junior point guard in Carey Rich and a journeyman sophomore in 6-8 Norm Greene upon which to build his foundation.

Watson, a gifted athlete, was playing under his third head coach in four years. Hall was in his second season of Division I competition after a two year junior college apprenticeship. Rich was beginning his second South Carolina season after transferring from Western Carolina, where he was Southern Conference Freshman of the Year.

Among the new players, 6-5 junior college transfer Andy Bostick and 6-9 Canadian freshman Peter Van Elswyck would become regulars. Junior college player Durrant Williams would play sparingly and leave after the season. Freshman Kelvin McClendon quit after five games. Freshman Donnie Mathews was hampered by a stress fracture and other injuries that would eventually curtail his career.

Despite all the tribulations, Fogler's team was competitive in most games but found victories hard to come by. Going into the season's final home game against Kentucky, the record was 7-18 with 10 of the losses coming by 6 points or less.

The Gamecocks lost by two points, 77-75, to a Florida team that wound up in the final four. South Carolina beat Alabama 82-66 in the season's ninth game, just before the Crimson Tide began a run to an NCAA bid.

The ease of the win over Alabama wasn't typical of the few victories earned. The Gamecocks went overtime to edge the College of Charleston and two overtimes before beating South Carolina State. A three point goal by Clemson came a second too late to send the game into overtime and South Carolina won 91-88.

South Carolina did claim two SEC wins over Tennessee, 64-62 and 72-64. The Gamecocks lost a heart breaker to Mississippi State, 73-72, and squandered a fifteen point second half lead in a loss to Georgia, 96-85. The other game with Georgia went down to the wire with Georgia eking out a 72-69 decision. Columbia native Ty Wilson came off the Bulldog bench to do the Gamecocks in with fourteen points in that one.

There weren't too many people on the planet who gave the Gamecocks much of a chance against seventh ranked Kentucky in the final Carolina Coliseum game of the 1994 season. South Carolina was 7-18, Kentucky was 23-5. Against Conference opponents, South Carolina was 3-12, the Wildcats 12-3.

It was a mismatch, but nobody told the Gamecocks.

Here's the way Stan Olson described it in the *Charlotte Observer*: "Of course— it came down to the final seconds—it had to. Kentucky guard Tony Delk had just put the Wildcats up 74-73 with a 9-foot jumper with 33 seconds left, and here came the Gamecocks one last time.

"South Carolina didn't call time out. Instead, Fogler called a one-four offensive set that gave senior Jamie Watson the ball at the top of the key and the freedom to make something happen.

"As the clock ran down, he passed the ball through Kentucky's trap to guard Carey Rich, who sliced into the lane from the left side. Fogler was yelling at Rich to shoot it, but Rich drew the defense to him and then caught senior Emmett Hall out of the corner of his eye.

"He bounced the ball to Hall, wide open under the basket. He easily laid it in with three seconds left."

South Carolina had done the impossible. The Gamecocks had beaten Kentucky 75-74. It was only the second victory in fifteen played against the Wildcats. South Carolina's 1932-33 team had split with Adolph Rupp's Wildcats, losing 44-36 at Lexington but winning 44-38 in Columbia enroute to a 17-2 record.

Jim Gilstrap's story in the Anderson *Independent-Mail* described it this way:

"A regular season of coming close ended Saturday afternoon when the University of South Carolina basketball team finally came through.

"Against Kentucky.

"Come again?

"Against seventh ranked KENTUCKY."

Gilstrap quoted point guard Carey Rich:

"Unbelievable, isn't it? You'd have to say its unbelievable."

Gilstrap called it "Unlikely. Unreal. Even unimaginable."

Many in the crowd of 10,638 poured onto the Frank McGuire Arena floor to join players in celebrating.

Emmett Hall hugged Jamie Watson and then leaped onto a chair and raised his arms in triumph. Hall had 20 points and 13 rebounds in the upset.

"I can't think of one any bigger than this," Hall told reporters. "I'll remember this the rest of my life."

Rich scored 19, a career high for him up to that point. He also had nine assists and committed only two turnovers. When Kentucky attempted a length of the court pass after Hall's basket with three seconds remaining, Watson batted the ball away. Rich grabbed it and threw it toward the coliseum rafters.

"All season long we've been in these situations," Watson said.

"Its not like we haven't known what to do, but the thing is, you've just got to do it."

The senior from Elm City, N. C., scored ten points in his final home game.

Watson set up the offense as Fogler decided against a time out before the final play. He received pressure from Kentucky defender Rodrick Rhodes and passed the ball to Rich on the right wing. Gimel Martinez came up to pressure Rich.

"I heard Coach Fogler yelling 'Hit it, hit it, so I started to penetrate with every intention of taking the shot," Rich recalled.

When Martinez came up, however, "I looked down low and saw Emmett. He was all alone."

Gilstrap noted that South Carolina scored on 17 of its last 18 possessions, including 14 in a row.

"Hall's layup punctuated one of South Carolina's greatest finishes against a team worthy of Kentucky's ranking," Gilstrap said.

The game began with South Carolina jumping off to an eight point lead, 11-3, after four and a half minutes, but Kentucky took the lead, 19-17, with nine minutes remaining and led by nine points, 34-25, at halftime

The Wildcat lead widened to 12 early in the second half but the Gamecocks kept battling back and Donnie Mathews' 22 foot 3 pointer with 5:24 left in the game cut Kentucky's lead to 3 at 61-58. Hall made 2 free throws to tie the score, 64-64, with 3:38 on the clock.

It was tied at 66, again at 67, and 69-69 before South Carolina grabbed the lead, 71-69, on two free throws by Mathews, with 1:50 left. A three pointer by Rodrick Rhodes put Kentucky back on top by a point, but Norm Greene's six footer gave the lead back to South Carolina, 73-72, at the 1:08 mark.

With 33 seconds remaining, Tony Delk scored from the baseline to put Kentucky ahead 74-73 and set the stage for Hall's dramatic game winner.

The win over Kentucky boosted Gamecock spirits as Fogler took his team to Memphis for the Southeastern Conference tournament in the Pyramid. In their two previous SEC tournaments, the Gamecocks had lost in the opening round, but riding the crest of the Kentucky win, South Carolina routed Mississippi by 23 points, 80-57.

In the quarter finals, however, Florida—on its way to a final four appearance—drubbed the Gamecocks 84-57 to end the Gamecock season.

XXXIII

South Carolina

vs

Georgia

January 28, 1995--South Carolina 60, Georgia 59

at Columbia

A leprechaun tipped it in.

Victories had been few and far between in the first two seasons of Eddie Fogler's rebuilding program at South Carolina. There was the thrilling one point home win over heavily favored Kentucky in Carolina Coliseum late in the 1993-94 season and the Gamecocks' first Southeastern Conference tournament victory, over Mississippi in the Pyramid at Memphis in March 1994.

Except for a few bright spots, Fogler was building for the future after taking over a talent and numbers depleted program following successful rebuilding stints at Wichita State and Vanderbilt.

Fogler's 1994-95 team, operating with only 8 scholarship players and 1 walk on, had struggled, winning only 4 times in 15 outings. With 1 or 2 exceptions, the Gamecocks had played hard and been competitive until fatigue set in and the opponent was able to take charge in the second half.

For example, South Carolina led defending NCAA champion Arkansas by four points, 42-38, at halftime Jan. 21 in Carolina Coliseum, only to wind up losing by fifteen, 88-73.

Five days later, the Gamecocks were able to notch their fourth win, a 22 point victory over Southern Conference leader Western Carolina, 90-68, an indication that the chemistry of Fogler's numbers shy squad was beginning to jell.

On the day the University of South Carolina paid tribute to legendary coach Frank McGuire and honored McGuire's greatest Gamecock team, a miracle shot with three seconds remaining delivered a one point victory over SEC rival Georgia.

Some said the spirit of McGuire nudged the final shot by Malik Russell into the basket. It seemed to teeter on the rim for a long long time before dropping through the nets. Perhaps the fact that Russell had transferred from Notre Dame after playing two seasons for the Fighting Irish and the pep band played "When Irish Eyes are Smil-

The 1975 South Carolina basketball team returned to Carolina Coliseum Jan. 28, 1995 for its 20th reunion sponsored by the USC Alumni Assn. *Front row (L-R):* Tom Riker, Billy Walsh, John Roche, Corky Carnevale, Rick Aydlett, Trainer Jim Price. *Back row:* John Ribock, Manager John Morganelli, Bob Carver, Tommy Terry, Dennis Powell, Administrative Asst. Ginger Rigdon, Broadcaster Bob Fulton, Gene Spencer, Sports Information Director Tom Price.—*USC Alumni Assn*

ing" in honor of McGuire's memory, had something to do with the way the game ended.

Georgia took a time out with two seconds showing on the clock. When the Bulldogs lined up to inbound the basketball, the Bulldogs looked over the Gamecock defense and called a 20 second time out under an experimental rule in Southeastern Conference games that allowed each team one 20 second time out per half. Georgia, which had saved all of its times out up to that point, attempted to "ice" the Gamecocks by taking two more times out.

After that war of nerves, Georgia managed to put the ball in play, but time ran out before the Bulldogs could get off a shot.

Final score, South Carolina 60, Georgia 59. The Gamecocks recorded their first SEC win of the season while Georgia saw its record drop to 12-5, 3-4 in the conference.

South Carolina jumped off to an 11 point halftime lead, 34-23, with a defense that limited Georgia to 30 per cent field goal accuracy in the first half on 9 field goals in 30 attempts. South Carolina shot a respectable 45.5 per cent on 15 of 33.

In the second half, the lack of depth showed itself and the Gamecocks shot only 25 per cent, 7 of 28. The 11 point lead disappeared and Georgia went ahead for the first time since the Bulldogs led 18-17 midway through the first half.

Georgia took the lead at 55-53 on Ty Wilson's three point goal with 4:11 remaining and the Bulldog lead grew to six points, 59-53, on two baskets by Steve Jones who had a perfect day, five for five, off the Georgia bench.

Carey Rich was fouled on a three point attempt and made two free throws for the Gamecocks. Freshman Melvin Watson pulled South Carolina to within one, 59-58, on a three point goal with 1:36 remaining.

Georgia's Pertha Robinson was fouled by Andy Bostick with thirty seven seconds remaining but missed the front end of a one and one attempt with Malik Russell claiming the rebound for South Carolina. The Gamecocks took a time out with twenty six seconds left.

Coach Fogler decided to play for the last shot trailing by one on his home floor, strategy that he would not normally employ.

"We decided to play for one shot at home, down by one. I don't know if I've ever done that before," he said in a post game interview.

"On the road I'd be happy to be down one with the ball. Usually, at home, you go the other way" and work for a good shot.

"I just decided that's something we'd try to do, try to get something at the buzzer. And, offensive rebounding is part of the last shot."

Bob Cole, writing in *The State*, described the final seconds:

"The play started with Russell at the top of the key in a 1-4 offense with Rich and (freshman Ryan) Stack on the wings. The hope was that Charles Claxton, Georgia's man mountain of a center, wouldn't be in the lane and Russell was to drive and try to create something.

"Claxton was there, however, and Russell dished it to Stack in the left corner. The idea was to take a 3-pointer, but he drove instead—'I don't know (why), just a feeling," he said—and got his baseline shot blocked. He (Stack) recovered the ball on the opposite side of the basket and flipped up what Russell referred to as 'some crazy kind of shot' that missed.

"Bostick and then, finally, Russell kept it alive in those frantic final seconds..." until Russell's tap hung on the rim and then toppled into the basket.

Cole noted "It might not have been as pretty as some of those wins by the 1969-70 team, but this edition of the Gamecocks couldn't have cared less."

Associated Press writer Pete Iacobelli quoted Russell, "that's three tons, this whole coliseum, off our back. We got the win. It's about time."

Rick Scoppe in the Greenville *News*, said "It was destiny. The Gamecocks would not dare lose to Georgia on the day the Gamecocks were honoring their all-time winningest coach."

South Carolina's 1970 basketball team, which compiled a 25-3 overall record and was 14-0 in regular season Atlantic Coast Conference games, attended the game in celebration of its 25th anniversary. That team was recognized with a halftime ceremony and post game reception, and a memorial tribute to McGuire—who died Oct. 11, 1994 at the age of 80—followed the game.

Players from 1970 who attended included Rick Aydlett, Corky Carnevale, Bob Carver, Dennis Powell, John Ribock, John Roche, Gene Spencer, Tommy Terry and Billy Walsh. Also present were team manager John Morganelli, assistant coach Bill Loving, trainer Jim Price, administrative assistant Ginger Rigdon and long time radio voice of the Gamecocks Bob Fulton.

Players unable to attend included Bobby Cremins, Billy Grimes and Tom Owens. Former assistant coach Donnie Walsh, president of the Indiana Pacers of the National Basketball Association, also was unable to attend.

Dr. John M. Palms, president of the University of South Carolina, Athletics Director, Dr. Mike McGee, former South Carolina governor Robert E. McNair, retired Episcopal rector, the Rev. John M. Barr, and two of McGuire's greatest players—John Roche and Alex English—paid tribute to Coach McGuire during the forty five minute ceremony.

McGuire's widow, Jane, and other members of the family also were present.

"It is very, very difficult to capture in a few minutes, in a few lines, the celebration of a very long, enjoyable life spent by someone doing what he wanted to do," Roche said as spokesman for the 25th anniversary team.

A three time All-America under McGuire and an attorney in Denver, Roche said McGuire "loved the association with his players, the competition of the games, the life of the basketball coach, the interaction with the fans and alumni."

Roche, an Academic All-America at South Carolina in addition to all-star recognition on the court, managed to graduate from law school while pursuing an eight year professional basketball career which ended with the Denver Nuggets. He said he would guess the most difficult day in McGuire's life was "the day he couldn't coach any more."

Former Gov. McNair called himself McGuire's "assistant recruiting coordinator" and said visiting recruits were frequently taken to the state capitol to be introduced to the governor.

"When Coach McGuire announced he was coming to South Carolina, there was more excitement than any one single thing I can recall," McNair said.

McGuire retired in 1980 after forty two seasons of coaching at the high school, college and professional levels. His total record was 725 wins and 305 losses. In thirty years at three universities—St. John's, North Carolina and South Carolina—his record was 550-235, including an undefeated NCAA championship team at North Carolina in 1957. His sixteen season record at South Carolina was 283-142.

English, the second African American to play basketball at South Carolina, and an accomplished poet in addition to other talents, recited a poem that he penned for the occasion.

He was a big city coach;
I was a skinny country kid.
He asked me to play;
that's what I did.
He said, "Come trail blaze a path
for others of your race."
We were civil rights comrades
in a non-civil rights place.
Your compassionate side
was most impressive to me.
It turned out to be
the most impressive lesson you'd teach.
For when you believed
you were standing for the right and truth,
your Irish stubbornness
would not let anything else through.
I consider myself lucky
to have played for the man.
And like the hundreds of your other players,
I will always be your fan.
He was a big city coach
who showed that he was just a man.

Index